Running
In and Around
Boston

Greg Wilmore

Ouizel Books
Cambridge, Massachusetts

Published by Ouizel Books
P.O. Box 2007
Osterville, MA 02655

Cover artwork by Matt Simon
Photographs were taken by the author.

ISBN 0-9655870-0-2
Library of Congress Catalog Card Number: 96-92941

Printed in the United States of America
First Edition/First Printing

Printed on recycled paper
containing twenty percent post-consumer fiber.

Acknowledgements

This book is a reservoir for a region overflowing with running lore. It is the by-product of towns where runners are eager to share their discoveries: a favorite neighborhood loop, a challenging sequence of hills, a quiet trail. For the runs in this book, I am no less indebted to this generosity of spirit than I am to the landscape itself, to the parks and forests, and to the people who fought to conserve these spaces for our enjoyment.

I would like to recognize the sources that helped produce this book. The United States Geological Survey provided the regional maps from which most of this book's graphics were derived. I am indebted to the Boston Public Library staff for their assistance with these documents. Pete Pfitzinger, in addition to writing the foreword, offered insightful comments that helped me improve the book. Tom Kennedy, of *Running Times*, also provided helpful tips. The Boston Athletic Association and the James Joyce Ramble both graciously granted permissions to use their race names in this book. I wish to thank the Peddie family and my friends at Marathon Sports for their professional advice and support.

My gratitude extends to the Birmingham family whose home served as my gateway to the western suburbs. Suzy, my savior, supplied a bike and computer. Marathon Maggie, my road tester, helped me see that my draft needed a good copy edit. Michael shared his Coke. As ever, I am indebted to my Wilmore family for all the years of love, and to Katie, for all our years to come.

Fifty Runs In and Around Boston

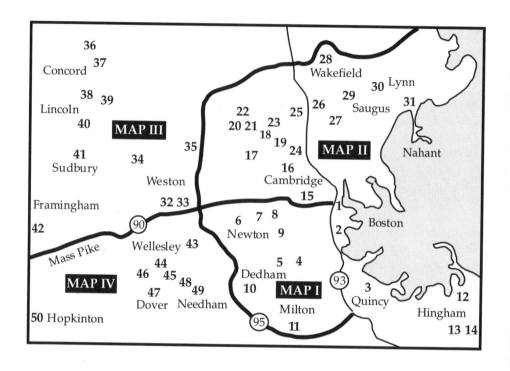

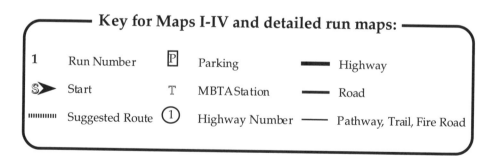

Key for Maps I-IV and detailed run maps:

1	Run Number	P Parking
S▶	Start	T MBTA Station
⁙	Suggested Route	① Highway Number

━━ Highway

━━ Road

━━ Pathway, Trail, Fire Road

Contents

Map III: The Northwestern Suburbs 79

Map IV: The Southwestern Suburbs 103

Appendices

Afterword 127

Foreword

The Boston area is the heart and soul of distance running in the United States. From the BAA Boston Marathon to the seclusion of Walden Pond, Boston and its environs offer a rich variety of roads, trails, hills and running companions. In the pages that follow, Greg Wilmore celebrates this diversity by presenting fifty of the most popular and inspiring running routes through Greater Boston.

When I moved to this area in 1979, I lived in a fourth floor apartment at Cleveland Circle on the marathon course. That apartment happened to be directly over the original Bill Rodgers Running Center. At that time, Bill used to run from the store several times a week with the likes of fellow marathoners Greg Meyer, Randy Thomas, and Bob Hodge. I would casually appear in front of the store to join them for a run around Jamaica Pond, over the Newton Hills, through the Arnold Arboretum, or along the Charles River, all at sub-six-minute-mile pace. Over the past two decades, I discovered the joy of running Fresh Pond (the world's most competitive fun run), the Weston Reservoir, Lake Waban, and many other loops highlighted in *Running In and Around Boston*.

Whether you are a seasoned veteran of the Boston running scene, or whether you have just arrived in the Hub, this guide will diversify your routine and enhance your enjoyment of running. For the native Bostonian looking for a new long run, you will find many tried and true options, complete with where to find water and toilets along the way. For the newcomer, you can avoid the potential pitfalls of exploring unfamiliar territory. For everyone, there are notes on the traffic, the hills, the scenery, and, for the fanatical, how to extend the length of the runs.

Make this guide your companion as you explore the many pleasures of running in the Boston area. I hope this information enriches your running experience. See you on the roads and trails in and around Boston!

Pete Pfitzinger

*Pete Pfitzinger was the first American
in the 1984 & 1988 Olympic Marathons.*

Introduction

When I first moved to Boston from San Francisco, I unpacked my shoes and set out in search of a good place to run. Of course, I had heard about the Charles River, so I started by looping around its banks and bridges. I became familiar with the pathways, found water and restrooms, and even met a few running companions. However, as the months and miles slipped by, the routine grew stale. I complained about the flatness of the river, and I waxed nostalgic for the golden hills of California. Wasn't there anywhere else to run in this town?

As you can imagine, my running partners defended the local scene. They invited me to join their club's track workouts and their expeditions away from the river. Thus began my true initiation to running in and around Boston. As we explored, I discovered why Boston has been called the hub of the solar system. It's all here: world famous races, scenic reservations, great meadows, the glaciated humps of Hingham. And yes--as we toiled over the Arlington Heights and the Newton Highlands--I was forced to admit that the region has hills upon hills.

Within a few years, I had a decent grasp of the landscape, but I was still getting to know Boston's runners. Here's a group that confronts severe storms, humid heat, rocky footing, and then seeks out any additional challenges the terrain has to offer. The courage and determination of our local heroes are well documented in books like Tom Derderian's *Boston Marathon*. Newcomers may be slow to pick up a Boston accent, but any runner is sure to be infected with enthusiasm for Boston's running lore.

Surrounded (as I was) by such a vibrant running community, and stuck (as I am) with a tendency to write things down, I decided to compile many of our favorite runs into this running guide. Whether you're a novice jogger exploring on weekends or a competitive athlete testing the upper limits of your heart rate monitor, this book has the roads and trails for you. The selections range from short to long, popular to remote, and flat to hilly. For each run, notes and maps indicate distances, surfaces, directions, facilities, elevation profiles, challenges, and intangibles.

Introduction

Runners who are unfamiliar with the region should locate specific runs using the maps, which are presented in three levels of detail. First, check the overall run distribution [p. 4]. Second, refer to the enlarged quadrant Maps I-IV that introduce each chapter: Boston and the Southeastern Suburbs, the Northeastern Suburbs, the Northwestern Suburbs, and the Southwestern Suburbs. Third, examine the detailed map presented for each run, and use the line-by-line directions to follow the suggested route. Note that these directions are not intended as a substitute for exploration.

Although this book is designed to provide accurate information about proven routes, it is also meant to guide you to those areas that are most likely to reward your wanderings. Please supplement this book's suggestions with your own experiences. Create new loops, combine runs, or tailor the routes to your own preferences. Remember, the best runs are often those that you discover accidentally. If running has become a chore, and you have memorized every crack in the sidewalk, then it could be time to explore beyond the sidewalk's end.

My fellow runners are some of the most contradictory people I know. I think this is why I find runners so intriguing. On the one hand we can be loners, and on the other hand we thrive on one another's company and competition. Some of the same parents who swear they jog to escape their children, nevertheless appear with their beloved offspring at the Arboretum's "Tot-Trot" race prepared to race hundreds of other baby-boomers-with-baby-joggers. We enjoy the city, but we find it hard to imagine life without the remarkable parks and green spaces. We set goals for the future, but we also embrace our past.

Of course you don't have to run the Freedom Trail to reenact history. You can do that on any route in this book as you follow in the footsteps of Patti Lyons Catalano, Joan Benoit Samuelson, and other local heroes. Make your own footsteps a part of this history. Leave tracks in the fresh snow. Add your heel strike to the trample at the start of a race. There is no better town for wearing down carbon-rubber outsoles. Boston is indeed the heart and soul of distance running, and we are the lifeblood. I hope this book helps you flow beyond the major arteries and into the complex networks of roads and trails that course through the body metropolis. Enjoy!

Summary Table

Run	Miles	Surface	Difficulty	Setting

Map I: Boston and the Southeastern Suburbs

Run	Miles	Surface	Difficulty	Setting
1. Boston Common	3.3	Path/road	Easy	Urban park
2. Pleasure Bay	8.2	Path/road	Moderate	Shoreline, urban
3. Quincy Shore	7.8	Road/path	Moderate	Town and shoreline
4. Franklin Park	4.2	Path/trial	Easy	Urban park
5. Arnold Arboretum	4.3	Path/trail	Moderate	Enormous garden
6. Newton Heights	11.5	Road	Variable	Tree-lined roads
7. Chestnut Hill	5.6	Path/road	Moderate	Reservoir running
8. Summit Ave	3.3	Road	Difficult	Residential
9. Emerald Necklace	10.4	Path/road	Moderate	Urban parks
10. James Joyce Ramble	6.2	Road	Moderate	Town and country
11. Blue Hills-West	6.0	Trail	Moderate	Wooded hills
12. World's End	3.9	Trail	Easy	Sculpted seascape
13. Wompatuck	7.2	Path/trail	Moderate	State forest
14. Whitney & Thayer	4.3	Trail	Moderate	Birch, evergreen

Map II: The Northeastern Suburbs

Run	Miles	Surface	Difficulty	Setting
15. Charles River	17.3	Path	Variable	Riverbanks
16. Fresh Pond	6.0	Path/road	Easy	Popular reservoir
17. Belmont Hill	4.3	Road/trail	Difficult	Scenic trail options
18. Arlington Heights	3.2	Road	Difficult	Panoramic views
19. Minuteman Trail	19.6	Path	Moderate	Bike path
20. Whipple Hill	3.8	Trail	Moderate	Wooded hillside
21. Lexington Meadow	--	Trail	Easy	Wetland
22. Four Corners	8.0	Road	Moderate	Residential hills
23. Mystic Lakes	5.0	Path/trail	Moderate	Lake loop
24. Somerville	6.8	Road/path	Difficult	Gutsy and gritty
25. Middlesex Fells	2.8	Trail	Easy	Mixed forest
26. Spot Pond	5.0	Road/trail	Moderate	Nature & freeway

Run	Miles	Surface	Difficulty	Setting

Map II (continued)

27. Melrose	8.3	Trail/road	Moderate	Park and town
28. Lake Quannapowitt	5.6	Path/road	Easy	Lakeside
29. Breakheart Res.	2.9	Path	Easy	Rolling hills
30. Lynn Woods Res.	4.9	Trail	Moderate	Oak, Pine, Maple
31. Nahant	8.6	Path/road	Moderate	Windy peninsula

Map III: The Northwestern Suburbs

32. Weston Reservoir	2.5	Trail	Easy	Mixed conifer
33. Doublet Hill	3.0	Trail	Difficult	Rocky upland trail
34. Cherry Brook	5.7	Trail	Moderate	Natural harmony
35. Hobbs Brooks Basin	6.0	Road	Moderate	Busy commercial
36. North Concord	10.4	Road/trail	Moderate	Historical
37. Great Meadows	3.6	Trail	Easy	Bird Heaven
38. Walden Pond	4.3	Trail	Moderate	Recreational
39. Sandy Pond	4.9	Trail	Moderate	Rugged pond loop
40. Mt. Misery	5.1	Trail	Moderate	Scenic and quiet
41. Sudbury River	13.5	Road/trail	Moderate	Rolling countryside
42. Callahan St. Forest	8.2	Trail/road	Moderate	State Forest

Map IV: The Southwestern Suburbs

43. Wellesley Forest	3.9	Trail/road	Moderate	Pond and fields
44. Lake Waban	8.1	Road	Moderate	Quiet residential
45. Elm Bank Res.	2.2	Trail	Easy	Secluded bliss
46. Natick	9.5	Road	Moderate	River and suburbs
47. Dover-Sherborn	12.9	Road/trail	Difficult	Fields and farms
48. Ridge Hill	2.6	Trail	Easy	Diverse wetlands
49. Needham Forest	1.4	Trail	Easy	Town forest
50. Boston Marathon	26.2	Road	Difficult	Suburban-busy

Charles River Esplanade

Map I: Boston and the Southeastern Suburbs

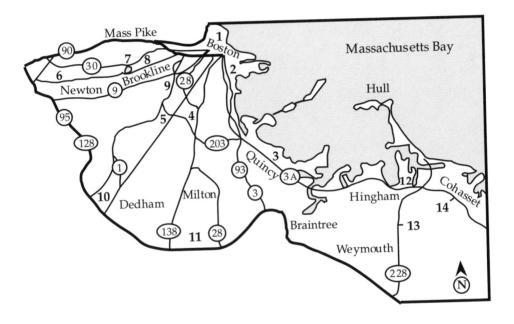

Boston State-house is the hub of the solar system.

- Oliver Wendell Holmes

Boston Common

Distances:	**Total Miles**	**3.3**
	Commonwealth Ave Loop	1.7

Surfaces: Paved pathway, grass median, sidewalk, and side of road.

Directions:

1. Start from the Park St MBTA station on the perimeter of Boston Common.
2. Run west through the center of the Common.
3. Continue across Charles St, and follow the bridge through the Public Garden.
4. Using the sidewalks or the mall, follow Commonwealth Ave out to Mass Ave and back to the edge of the Garden.
5. Turn left onto Arlington St.
6. Turn right onto Beacon St.
7. Turn left onto Charles St.
8. Turn right onto Pinckney St.
9. Turn right onto Joy St and descend the Guild Steps into the Common. Bear left to return to the start.

Notes: The stately elegance of Boston Common, Back Bay and Beacon Hill will seduce visitors and rekindle civic passions among city dwellers. Although the Common is often packed with human obstacles, several alternate paths are available. Runners may also follow Mass Ave north to the river, or continue two blocks south and west of Mass Ave to reach the Back Bay Fens [p. 30].

Facilities: Restrooms are available in businesses on Charles St. Water is available at various points along the Charles River [pp. 44-45].

Map I: Boston and the Southeastern Suburbs

3.3 miles

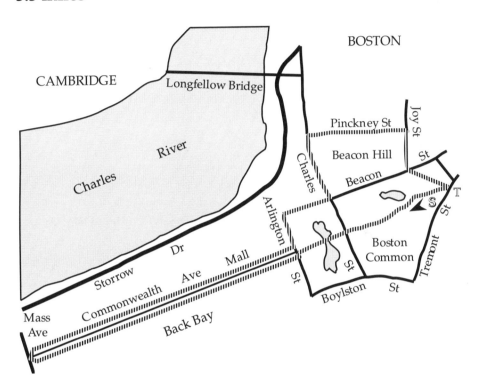

CAMBRIDGE

BOSTON

Longfellow Bridge

Charles River

Charles

Pinckney St

Joy St

Beacon Hill

St

Beacon

Boston Common

Arlington

St

St

Dr

Mall

Ave

Storrow

Commonwealth

Boylston

St

Tremont

St

Mass Ave

Back Bay

Hill Profile

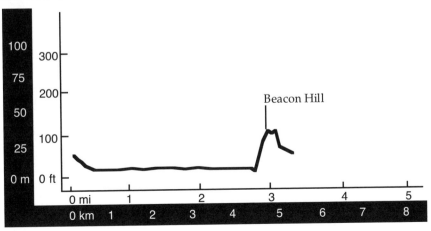

Beacon Hill

Pleasure Bay

Distances:	**Total Miles**	**8.2**
	Pleasure Bay Loop	2.2
	Columbus Park Loop	1.5
	Columbia Point (out & back)	1.7

Surfaces: Paved pathway, sidewalk, side of road. Beach optional.

Directions:
1. Start at Carson Beach parking area on Day Blvd.
2. Run north along the edge of Columbus Park and cross Columbia Rd to Old Harbor St.
3. Run uphill and turn right onto Telegraph Hill.
4. Turn left onto G St.
5. Turn right onto East Broadway.
6. Turn right onto M St. Follow M St to the L St Beach, turn left, and follow shoreline to the Head Island Causeway.
7. Loop around Pleasure Bay and return along Columbia Rd, Day Blvd or the beach.
8. Loop around Columbus Park and return to the start.
9. Follow the shoreline path to Columbia Point and back.

Notes: As the aptly named Pleasure Bay suggests, South Boston is a great place to relax in the summer. One runner loops out from the city in search of a cool breeze. Another checks out Castle Island and the JFK building. Nobody (except maybe the occasional L-Street die-hard) goes to Paul Saunders Stadium to hammer out a PR. The most athletic displays should be reserved for public consumption along the beach.

Facilities: Restrooms are available at the L St bathhouse. Water fountains are located at several points along the shoreline.

Map I: Boston and the Southeastern Suburbs

8.2 miles

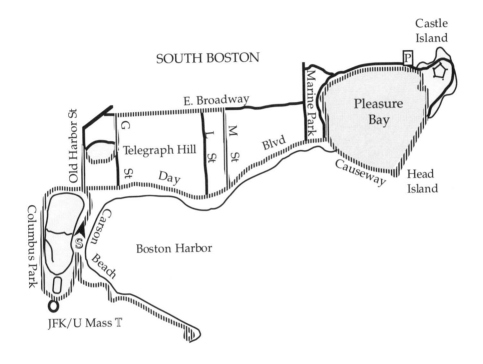

SOUTH BOSTON

Castle Island

P

Marine Park

Pleasure Bay

E. Broadway

Old Harbor St

G St

Telegraph Hill

L St

M St

Blvd

Causeway

Head Island

St

Day

Columbus Park

Carson Beach

S

Boston Harbor

JFK/U Mass T

Hill Profile

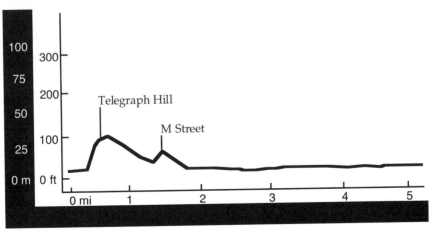

100	300
75	200
50	100
25	
0 m	0 ft

Telegraph Hill

M Street

0 mi   1   2   3   4   5

Quincy Shore

Distances:	**Total Miles**	7.8

Surfaces: Paved pathway, sidewalk, and side of road. Sand is also an option at Wollaston Beach.

Directions:
1. Start from the parking area on Quincy Shore Dr.
2. Run south and turn right onto Furnace Brook Pkwy.
3. Turn right onto Newport Ave.
4. Turn left onto South Central Ave.
5. Turn left onto Summit Ave to run over Forbes Hill.
6. Descend and turn left onto Beale St.
7. Turn right onto Adams St.
8. Merge right onto Granite Ave.
9. Turn right onto Squantum St.
10. Cross Hancock St and continue on East Squantum St.
11. Turn right onto Quincy Shore Dr and return to start.

Notes: This run sticks to the edges of a park, a golf course, a town, and finally, the edge of a cool-gray ocean. Runners should stick to the edges as well to avoid commercial and beach-related traffic. The terrain is as varied as the scenery. Forbes Hill coils out of the flat salt marshes like a hissing serpent. Squantum St also offers a generous sampling of the region's rolling hills. In fact, runners who continue a quarter mile eastward on East Squantum St can explore the short wood trail around Moswetuset Hummock. Continue another mile farther to visit Chapel Rock.

Facilities: Water is available from fountains along Wollaston Beach.

Map I: Boston and the Southeastern Suburbs

7.8 miles

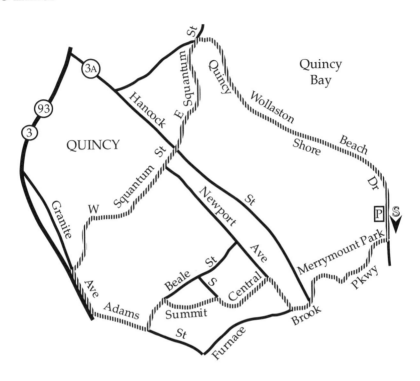

Hill Profile

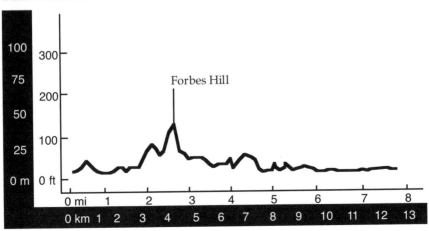

Franklin Park

Distances:	**Total Miles**	**4.2**
	Circuit Drive Loop	2.6
	Playstead (Stadium) Loop	1.2

Surfaces: Paved pathway, dirt trail, and grass trail.

Directions:
1. Start at the courts between Morton St and Circuit Dr.
2. Follow the road that winds up Scarborough Hill.
3. Loop along the stone wall and return downhill.
4. Turn left and follow a path alongside the golf course; continue across a bridge over Scarborough Pond.
5. Turn left and follow Circuit Dr around the golf course to the central interchange. Cross Circuit Dr and turn right (as if headed toward the Zoo). Continue around the perimeter of the fields and then turn right up into Crouch Woods.
6. Descend, run around White Stadium, and follow the grass path back toward the central interchange.
7. As you approach the interchange make a hairpin right turn and follow the grass path along a stone wall.
8. Follow the cross-country path through the Wilderness, cross Circuit Dr and turn right to return to start.

Notes: Anyone who has raced over the park's cross-country course will have no difficulty imagining a ghost crowd of spectators yelling encouragement and hovering like their own breath on the crisp autumn air. Those voices from the glory days may echo sadly as they bounce off the ruins, the empty stadium, and the old Zoo cages, but the message is clear: shake off the rust. You're back in Zoom Country!

Facilities: Restrooms and water are available at the golf shop and the Franklin Park Zoo.

4.2 miles

Hill Profile

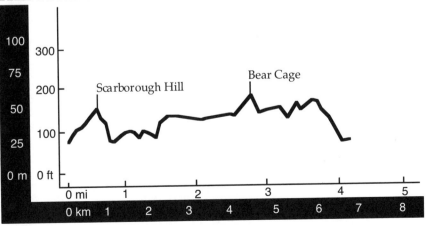

Arnold Arboretum

Distances:	**Total Miles**	**4.3**
	To Jamaica Pond [p. 30]	0.7
	To Franklin Park [p.20]	1.7

Surfaces: Paved pathway and trails.

Directions:
1. Start on Sargent Trail near the Visitor's Center.
2. Follow the trail to Hill Rd, turn right, and continue to Valley Rd. Start down, then turn right onto Conifer Path.
3. Follow Conifer Path to end. Turn right out to Walter St, then make a hairpin left (back into park) onto Bussey Rd.
4. Turn right to Peters Hill Rd. Loop around to back of hill ascend and descend path to hilltop, then complete loop.
5. Cross Bussey St and continue on Hemlock Hill Rd.
6. Turn right to rejoin Sargent Trail which climbs steeply to an overlook and then descends sharply to a stream.
7. Turn left and then cross a footbridge over the stream.
8. Continue up Valley Rd, then turn right onto Beech Path.
9. Following the "no-bicycle" signs, bear left onto Oak Path, then right onto Chinese Path. Rejoin the road which curls up to the top of Bussey Hill.
10. Descend Hill Rd, loop past Rehder Pond, and return to the start on Meadow Rd.

Notes: Runners may be moving too fast to absorb the abundant detail on individual species but they won't miss the big-picture: views of the arboretum itself, the Boston skyline, and, in May, the intoxicating bloom of lilacs.

Facilities: Restrooms are available at the Visitor's Center. Water is located at the intersection of Hill and Valley roads.

4.3 miles

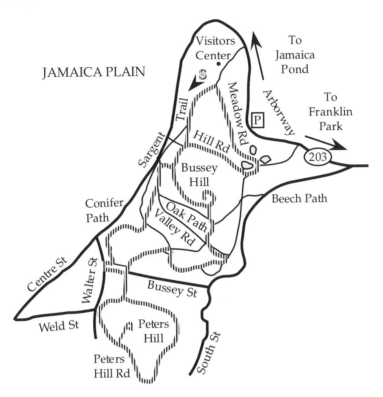

Hill Profile

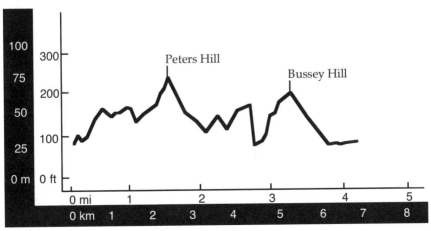

Newton Hills

Distances:	**Total Miles**	**11.5**
	Centre Street Loop	5.3
	Walnut Street Loop	6.8
	Chestnut Street Loop	8.8

Surfaces: Sidewalk, road shoulder, and side of road.

Directions: 1. Start at Cleveland Circle (east of the Chestnut Hill Reservoir) and run west on Beacon St.
2. Turn right onto Washington St.
3. At the fire station, turn right onto Commonwealth Ave. Note the availability of the access road and grass median.
4. Bear right onto Chestnut Hill Ave.
5. Continue downhill to the start.

Notes: If you run this loop clockwise, you'll bump up against the Boston Marathon's notorious Heartbreak Hill. Like the fish that got away, Hyperbolic Hill seems to get a little bit bigger with each retelling. Sure, it's tough, but if you're into real cardiac crisis, take a spin up Waban Hill Rd which departs from the top of Heartbreak. For fewer miles, try the cutoffs listed above. For additional miles, merge this route with the Chestnut Hill run [p. 26], the Summit Ave run [p. 28], or the Boston Marathon [p. 118]. There are also two worthwhile detours south of Beacon St; the first, Hammond Pond Park Reservation off of Hammond Pond Parkway; the second, Cold Springs Park off of Winslow Rd.

Facilities: Restrooms and water are available at the Chestnut Hill MDC facility. Water is available at the Alumni field (off Beacon St) and in City Hall (on Commonwealth Ave).

11.5 miles

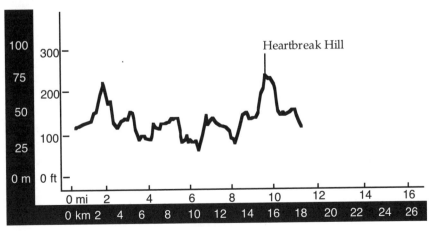

Hill Profile

Chestnut Hill & Brookline Reservoirs

Distances:	**Total Miles**	**5.6**
Chestnut Hill Reservoir	1.6
Chestnut Hill Ave (out)	1.1
Brookline Reservoir	0.9
Fisher Ave (back)	2.0
To Summit Ave run	0.7

Surfaces: Paved pathway, sidewalk, and side of road.

Directions:
1. Start at Chestnut Hill Park near Cleveland Circle.
2. Run around the Reservoir and wind through a Parcourse.
3. Descend the brief hill to Beacon St and turn left to reach Cleveland Circle.
4. Turn right onto Chestnut Hill Ave; proceed over the hill.
5. Use caution crossing Route 9, turn left and descend a bank to Brookline Reservoir.
6. Loop around Brookline Reservoir and recross Route 9.
6. Follow Route 9 a block east and turn left onto Fisher Ave.
7. Run over the hill and turn left onto Clinton Rd.
8. Bear left onto Eliot, then right onto Cleveland Rd.
9. Turn right onto Crafts Rd, then right onto Reservoir Rd.
10. Cross Beacon St with care and turn right to the start.

Notes: This course alternates flat loops with challenging grades. If the grand roosts of Brookline whet your appetite for hills, help yourself to seconds by following Beacon St to the Summit Ave run [p. 28]. For a third reservoir, venture south and loop Jamaica Pond [p. 30].

Facilities: Restrooms and water are available at the Chestnut Hill MDC facility. Water is available at Alumni Field.

5.6 miles

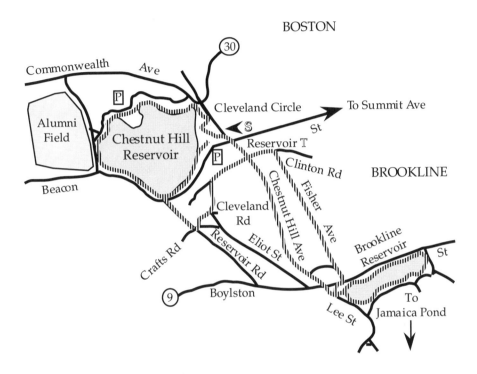

Hill Profile

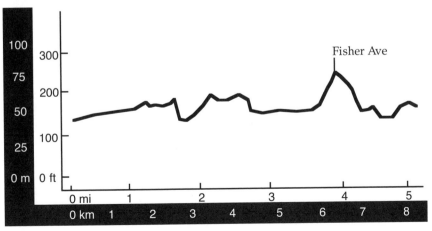

Summit Ave

Distances:	**Total Miles**	**3.3**
	to Chestnut Hill run	0.7

Surfaces: Sidewalk, side of road, and stairways.

Directions:
1. Start on Beacon St at Winthrop Rd; run up Winthrop Rd.
2. Turn right up Addington Path (stairway A on the map).
3. Turn right onto Addington Rd, then left down Claflin Path (B). Turn left onto Claflin Rd.
4. Merge left onto Rawson Rd.
5. Bear left onto Colbourne Cres.
6. Turn left up Colbourne Path (C).
7. Turn right onto Addington.
8. Turn left onto Colbourne Cres.
9. Turn right onto Winthrop.
10. In quick succession, turn left onto Gardner Rd, right onto Hancock Rd, then left down Gardner Path (D).
11. Turn right onto Washington St
12. Turn left onto Park St.
13. Cross Beacon St, turn left and continue to Summit Ave.
14. Run over the hill and turn left onto Corey Rd.
15. Turn left onto Williston Rd.
16. Turn left onto Beacon St and return to the start.

Notes: Warm up along Beacon St before tackling the hills and staircases. With quaint paths like these, who needs a stationary stair machine? Don't miss early opportunities to slurp up both water and scenery. Fortify your brain and gut, and hope that neither abandons you on Corey Hill.

Facilities: Water is available at Schick Park (at the top of Addington Path), St Mark's Square, and the Corey Hill Outlook.

3.3 miles

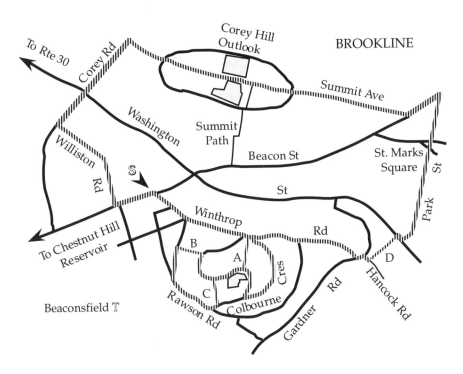

Hill Profile

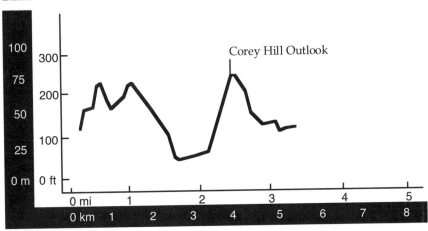

The Emerald Necklace

Distances:	**Total Miles**	**10.4**
	Jamaica Pond Loop	1.4

Surfaces: Paved pathway, sidewalk, and side of road.

Directions:
1. Start at the Back Bay Fens south of the Charles River.
2. Run west on the paved path that follows Park Drive.
3. At the Sears Building, turn left onto the path that follows the Muddy River south.
4. Turn right onto Netherlands Rd.
5. Turn left onto Parkway Rd and right onto Brookline Ave.
6. Turn right onto Washington and right onto Pond Ave.
7. Bear left onto Riverdale Parkway (or onto the path).
8. Turn left onto Perkins St; continue onto Goddard Rd.
9. Turn left onto Newton St, then left into Anderson Park.
10. Turn left onto Avon.
11. Right on Goddard Rd. (Return to path around pond).
12. Return north alongside Olmsted Park (Jamaicaway).
13. At intersection with Washington St, cross and continue on River Rd. Continue on path alongside Brookline Ave.
14. Turn left onto path or sidewalk alongside Riverway.
15. Return alongside Fenway to the start.

Notes: Olmsted's Emerald Necklace strings together the Back Bay Fens, Olmsted Park, Jamaica Pond and Anderson Park. The route is level, but the roads to Anderson Park rise and dip over a span of 150 ft. For the missing jewels, see Franklin Park [p. 20] and Arnold Arboretum [p. 22].

Facilities: Restrooms are available at Anderson Park, the Jamaica Pond Boathouse, and off of Fenway. Water is available from a fountain at the north end of Jamaica Pond.

Map I: Boston and the Southeastern Suburbs

10.4 miles

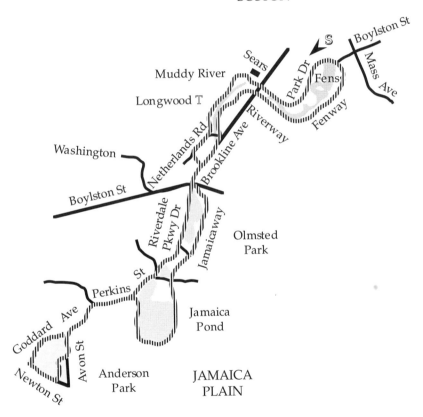

James Joyce Ramble

Distances: | **Total Miles** | **6.2**

Surfaces: Sidewalk, road shoulder, and side of road.

Directions:
1. Start in front of Dedham's VFW building on Eastern Ave.
2. Cross Route 1 and turn left onto High St.
3. Bear left onto Church St.
4. Turn left onto Court St.
5. Turn right onto Highland St.
6. Turn right onto Lowder St.
7. Turn right onto High St which becomes Bridge St.
8. Turn left into Nobles campus and follow Campus Dr.
9. Exit at school's entrance and turn right onto Pine St.
10. Pine St becomes Ames St. Follow Ames St to High St.
11. Turn left onto High St which dips under Route 1.
12. Bear right onto East St, and turn left onto Whiting Ave.
13. Turn right onto Mt Vernon St.
14. Turn right into Endicott Estate (just after Walnut St).
15. Turn right onto East St.
16. Turn left down Eastern Ave to Dedham Square.

Notes: If you're not racing this popular 10 km, then you'll have time to appreciate the colonial houses, the river, the Nobelonian trails, and the historic town buildings. If, however, Dedham's flavors seem either overpowered or intensified by a crowd of joyful runners, and if you encounter Joyce-readers, Irish musicians, bagpipes, refreshments, literary trivia and a Human Rights Dedication, then it's probably race day.

Facilities: Restrooms and water are available at Dedham Sq. A gas station is located at Ames St.

6.2 miles

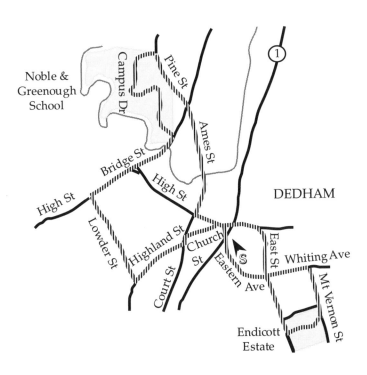

Hill Profile

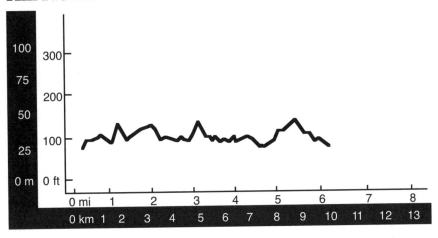

Blue Hills-West

Distances: | **Total Miles** | **6.0**
Summit Rd | 1.0

Surfaces: Dirt pathway, paved pathway (Bugbee Path), and road shoulder (Unquity Rd).

Directions:
1. Start from the parking lot north of Trailside Museum.
2. Follow Wolcott Path to the Reservation Headquarters.
3. Cross Chickatawbut Rd to Bugbee Path.
4. At marker 2070, turn right and continue downhill to Houghtons Pond. Circle the pond and follow Headquarters Path (alongside Chickatawbut Rd) to complete the loop.
5. Merge left onto Unquity Rd.
6. Turn left onto Chestnut Run Path.
7. Turn left onto Border Path.
8. Turn left onto Bartol Path.
9. At Five Corners intersection, turn right on Wolcott Path and return to start.

Notes: The suggested route passes over mostly level terrain. However, the Reservation's 7,000 acres offer loops for runners of all abilities and agilities. Macho runners train on Big Blue's (635 ft.) steep ski slopes and Summit Rd. Come race day, anyone with antelope ancestory and mountain-goat ankles can hope to survive the competition over the nasty, brutish (and not-so-short) Skyline Trail. Check the maps posted at the Reservation for directions to Ponkapoag Pond and the eastern Blue Hills.

Facilities: Restrooms and water available at Trailside Museum and Houghton's Pond. Water is available at the Reservation Headquarters.

Map I: Boston and the Southeastern Suburbs

6.0 miles

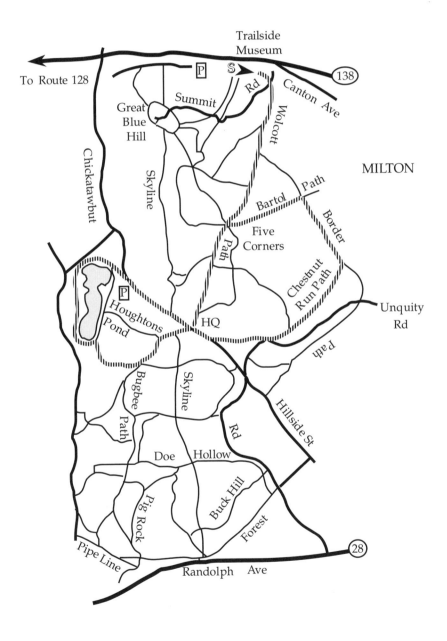

World's End

Distances:	**Total Miles**	**3.9**

Surfaces: Dirt and grass pathways. Rocky Neck is aptly named.

Directions:
1. Start from the top parking area inside the Reservation.
2. Follow the gravel path counter-clockwise and turn right onto a dirt trail to tour Rocky Neck.
3. Return to the main trail and turn right. Follow the trail to the isthmus and cross to the northern land mass.
4. Circle the northern projection and return over the same causeway.
5. Continue straight onto the path that climbs the face of Pine Hill, then bear left and descend the opposite side of the hill.
6. Rejoin the perimeter trail and return to the start.

Notes: Admission is $3.50, and this is a pain in the Achilles. Running should be cheap. Sure, we hemorrhage millions into the Nike coffers, but that's not the point. We like to roam free on principle. Nevertheless, it's worth a half-hour drive and a few bucks to experience World's End.

Everything about World's End suggests motion, from the peninsula's amoeboid projections to the Olmsted-designed trails. As you follow a line of trees over the glacially carved drumlins, a seamless seascape scrolls across your bow. You can stop to take in the views, but the waves keep lapping all around, and the world just seems to keep on spinning on it's end.

Facilities: Portable toilets are located next to the lower parking area. No drinking water is available.

Map I: Boston and the Southeastern Suburbs

3.9 miles

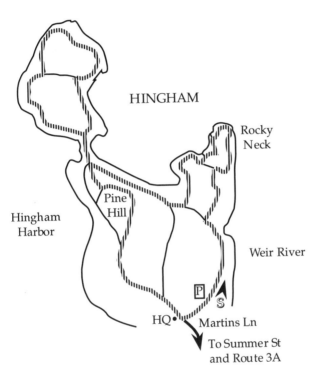

Hill Profile

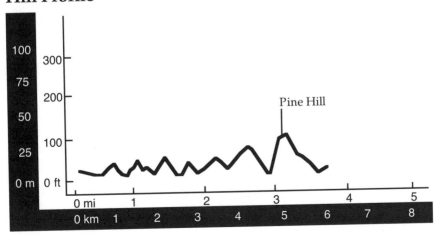

Wompatuck State Forest

Distances:	**Total Miles**	**7.2**
	Combined with Whitney & Thayer	11.5

Surfaces: Paved pathway and dirt trail (Nature Area).

Directions:
1. Start on the paved road opposite the Visitor Center.
2. Pass through a gate. Follow the pathway (first right and then left) in a southeasterly direction. Continue on the "bike trail"alongside an abandoned railroad. Rejoin the paved pathway and continue out of the gated area.
3. Merge with bicycle path and continue to an intersection.
4. Turn left and then left again to begin a "square" loop.
5. Turn right and then right again to complete square.
6. Turn left and complete Nature Loop. (The Hill Profile is recorded in a clockwise direction).
7. Rejoin the road and continue straight, passing Heron Pond and Aaron Reservoir.
8. Before reaching Union St, turn right near the top of the hill onto the bicycle path and zig-zag back to the start.

Notes: Since Wompatuck was once a munitions depot, it should come as no surprise that this forest has an ample supply of asphalt and concrete. Ironically, this is part of the park's appeal; the smooth and rolling pathways lure in-line skaters, bikers and runners. Still, runners who don't mind a few rocks and roots can explore the untamed footpaths. For additional trail miles, continue east past the Nature Study Area and join the Whitney Woods run [p. 40].

Facilities: Restrooms and water are available at the Visitor Center.

7.2 miles

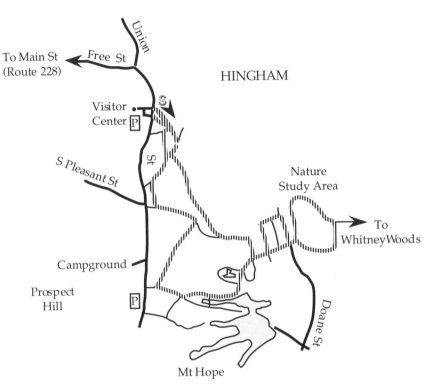

Hill Profile

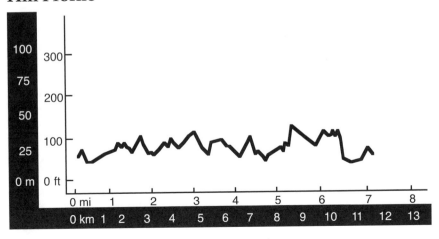

Whitney & Thayer Woods

Distances: **Total Miles**   **4.3**
Combined with Wompatuck   11.5

Surfaces: Unpaved roads and pathways with a stretch of very rocky terrain on Thayer Trail (from marker 13 to 16).

Directions: 1. Start from the main parking area (opposite Sohier St).
2. At marker 1, turn right onto Boulder Lane.
3. At marker 7, turn right onto Whitney Rd.
4. At marker 11, turn left and continue to marker 13.
5. At marker 13, turn off the main path onto a footpath.
6. Cross an abandoned railroad bed, pass through Holly Grove and ascend to marker 16.
7. At marker 16, turn left onto One Way Lane.
8. At marker 17, turn left onto James Hill Lane.
9. Continue past marker 18 onto Milliken Memorial Path.
10. Continue past markers 19, 20, 21 and 22. The trail then passes a private residence before returning to the start.

Notes: Over the ages, these woods have been scraped by glaciers, cleared for farming, and run through by a railroad, but the last century has witnessed a detente. From Turkey Hill (187 ft.), a runner sees that the conifers have grown back as thick and tall as the armada of masts in Cohasset Harbor. For additional miles, runners may explore some of the more precarious footpaths (Bancroft and Thayer Trails) or join the Wompatuck run [p. 38]. The path to Wompatuck's Nature Study Area departs south from marker 19.

Facilities: There are neither restrooms (other than the ample and obvious outdoor options) nor water fountains, but there is a shopping area opposite the entrance to Thayer Woods.

4.3 miles

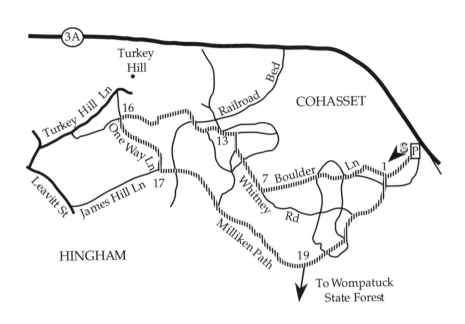

Hill Profile

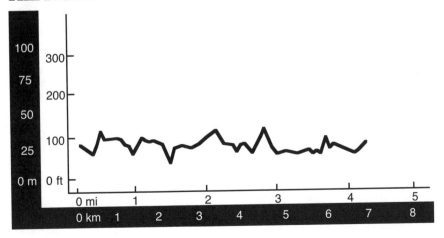

Lake Quannapowitt, Wakefield

Map II: The Northeastern Suburbs

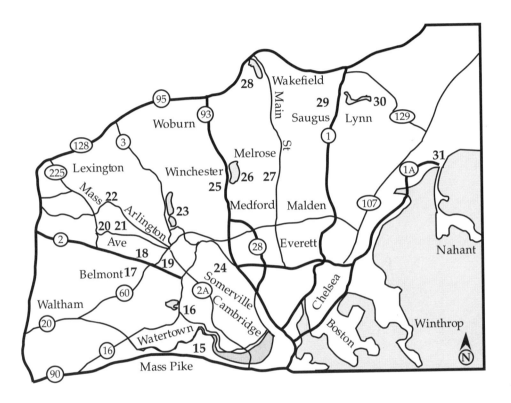

Crossing a bare common, in snow puddles, at twilight, under a clouded sky, without having in my thoughts any occurence of special good fortune, I have enjoyed a perfect exhilaration.

- Ralph Waldo Emerson

Charles River

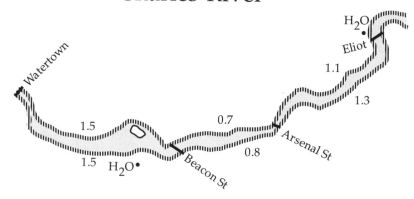

Distances: Between-bridge mileages are shown above, and bridge loop distances are listed in the chart at right.

Surfaces: A paved pathway circles the river, and dirt trails are available over most of the route.

Notes: The River's popular orbitals embrace runners, skaters, strollers and bikers. We may tire of the flatness, and we may even tire of one another, but we keep coming back to work on our pacing, to put in the long miles, and--oh yes-- for those plain old fun in the sun runs. Every Sunday during the warmer months, the parks department closes Memorial Drive to traffic from Western Ave to Eliot Bridge between 11 A.M. and 7 P.M. There's no ice or freezing rain, but it's still a cool scene for the recreationally hip.

Facilities: Restrooms are available at the Science Museum and the Daly Memorial Skating Rink. During the summer, Lee Pool and the Charles River Reservation facilities may also be used. Water fountain locations are shown above as "H_2O."

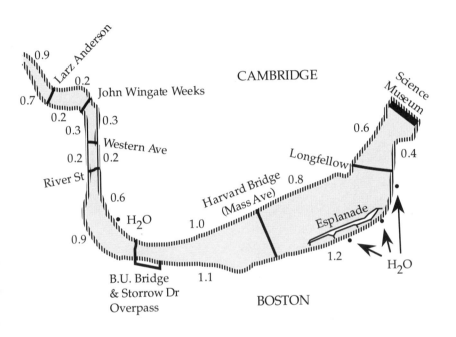

BRIDGE LOOP DISTANCES
(miles/kilometers)

	Beacon	Arsenal	Eliot	Anderson	Weeks	Western	River	B.U.	Harvard	Longfellow	Science Museum
Longfellow											1.7/2.8
Harvard										2.8/4.6	3.7/6.0
B.U.									2.7/4.3	4.7/7.6	5.6/9.0
River								2.1/3.4	4.1/6.6	6.1/9.8	7.0/11.3
Western							0.6/1.0	2.5/4.1	4.5/7.2	6.5/10.5	7.7/12.4
Weeks						0.8/1.3	1.2/2.0	3.1/5.1	5.1/8.2	7.1/11.5	8.3/13.3
Anderson					0.7/1.1	1.3/2.1	1.7/2.8	3.7/5.9	5.6/9.0	7.6/12.3	8.8/14.2
Eliot				1.8/2.9	2.3/3.7	2.9/4.7	3.4/5.4	5.3/8.5	7.2/11.6	9.2/14.9	10.4/16.8
Arsenal			2.6/4.2	4.2/6.8	4.7/7.6	5.3/8.6	5.8/9.3	7.7/12.4	9.6/15.5	11.7/18.8	12.8/20.7
Beacon		1.7/2.7	4.1/6.6	5.7/9.2	6.2/10.1	6.8/11.0	7.2/11.7	9.2/14.8	11.1/17.9	13.6/22.0	14.3/23.1
Watertown	3.0/4.9	4.7/7.6	7.1/11.4	8.7/14.0	9.2/14.8	9.8/15.8	10.2/16.5	12.1/19.5	14.1/22.7	16.1/26.0	17.3/27.8

Fresh Pond

Distances:	**Total miles**	**6.0**
	Cambridge Common Loop	0.45
	Fresh Pond Loop	2.25

Surfaces: Paved pathway and sidewalk.

Directions:
1. Start at Cambridge Common just north of Harvard Sq.
2. Run around the Common to Concord Ave.
3. Cross Garden St at Arsenal Sq.
4. At the top of the hill, turn left onto Huron Ave.
5. Cross to Fresh Pond and complete the loop.
6. Return to the start via Fresh Pond Parkway and Concord Ave, or detour through Denehy Park and return on Garden St.

Notes: Keep Fresh Pond fresh by jumping from the paved path onto the trails. Use caution when crossing the busy streets that border the pond. Emergency call boxes and lights are scattered around the pond. However, at night, stretches of the pathway are still quite dark. Also, join the informal Saturday morning (10 A.M.) runs which consist of two loops around the pond and Kingsley Park. If all else fails to put a spring in your swollen feet, blame the shoes, and end your run at the Marathon Sports on Mass Ave where a staff of runners will fit you to shoes that match to your mechanics.

Facilities: Restrooms and water are available at the Fresh Pond Golf Shop, Denehy Park, and Marathon Sports. Water is available at the Athletic Field (south of the pond) and at Kingsley Park (east of the pond).

6.0 miles

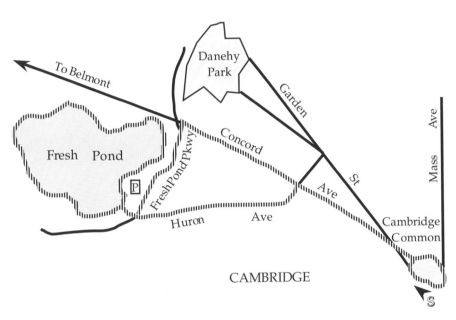

Hill Profile

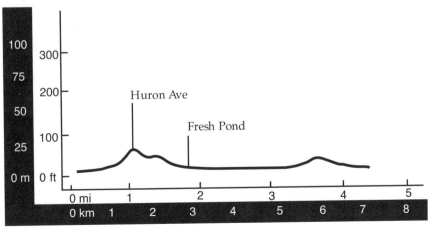

Belmont Hill

Distances:	**Total Miles**	**4.3**
	Using Concord Ave	4.6

Surfaces: Sidewalk and side of road. Trail optional.

Directions:
1. Start at Beaver Brook Reservation on Mill St.
2. Turn left out of parking area onto Mill St.
3. Bear left onto Concord Ave.
4. Turn right onto Marsh St.
5. Bear right onto Prospect and Clifton Streets.
6. Turn right at signal onto Pleasant Street.
7. [Hill option: make a hairpin right turn onto Concord Ave, then turn left on Mill St to return to start].
8. Turn right onto Trapello Rd.
9. Turn right onto Mill St.

Notes: As the hill profile suggests, the character of this run changes as you switch directions. For example, the steep descent at Clifton St becomes an extended climb. Either way, it's a tough run, and humping it over Concord Ave makes it even tougher. Pleasant St isn't all that pleasant, but it's relatively flat, and that may be a welcome break from all the acutely angled scenery. Adventurers will discover several good trail romps in the area including (but not limited to) Rock Meadow Conservation area and the hospital grounds.

Facilities: Restrooms and water are available at Beaver Brook Reservation (immediately south of Trapello Rd), in gas stations along Pleasant St, and at the intersection of Concord Ave and Mill St.

4.3 miles

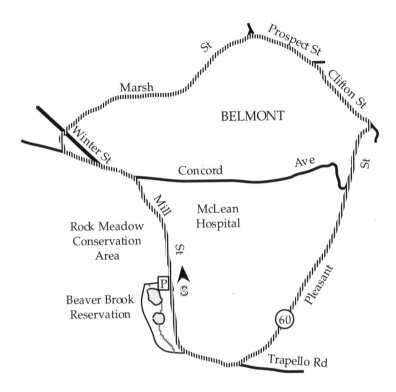

Hill Profile

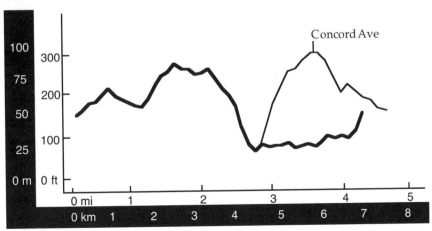

Arlington Heights

Distances:	**Total Miles**	**3.2**

Surfaces: Dirt pathway, sidewalk, and side of road.

Directions:
1. Start in Menotomy Rocks Park at Hills Pond.
2. Run to exit at southwestern corner of park and turn left onto Old Spring St. At first right, turn onto Arlmont St.
3. Proceed uphill and turn right onto Scituate St.
4. Turn left onto Eastern Ave and continue up to Park Tower.
5. At Park Circle, turn right and descend on Cedar St.
6. Turn right onto Oakland Ave.
7. Turn right onto Appleton St.
8. Turn right onto Harvard St. Continue to end of road and follow paved pathway up through wooded lot to Gray St.
8. Turn left onto Gray St, then right onto Grandview Rd.
9. At the top of the incline, turn left onto Spring Ave, an unmarked lane that runs downhill, narrows to a pathway, and finally becomes High Haith.
10. At Ottawa Rd, turn left into Menotomy Rocks and follow the pathway down the to start at Hills Pond.

Notes: This is a short course, but the slopes are black diamond material. The view from Robbins Farm provides the excuse you may (not) need to pause in the steep ascent to Park Tower. If you're a hill fanatic, the Heights should test your zeal.

Facilities: Hope that Public Works fixes the fountain at Hills Pond and try to ignore the looming irony of Park Tower Public Water Supply's two million gallons of water as you die of thirst. Facilities and water are located inside Ottoson School.

3.2 miles

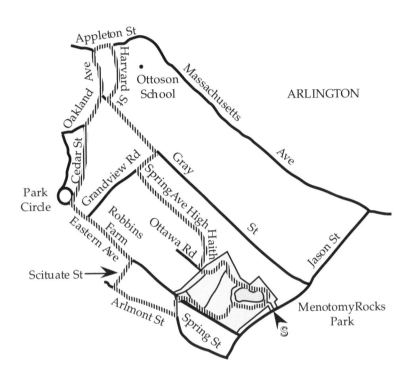

Hill Profile

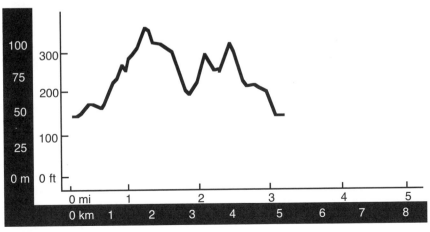

Minuteman Trail

Distances: **Total Miles (out & back)   19.6**

Surfaces: Paved pathway.

Directions:
1. Start at the end of Varnum St (north of Alewife station).
2. Follow the trail just over a mile to the intersection of Mass Ave with Pleasant and Mystic Streets.
3. Cross to the Mystic side of the intersection where the trail resumes.
4. The trail follows the old Boston & Maine Railroad bed to Bedford. Use caution when crossing the many roads that intersect the path.

Notes:
Myth: the Minuteman Trail is flat.
Fact: okay, it's not Mt. Washington, but the trail offers a hearty (if gradual) climb and descent.

Myth: the Minuteman is a straight, boring out-back.
Fact: okay, it's not tortuous, but if you tire of the gentle bends, jump off-trail and explore Parker Meadow, Arlington Reservoir, Whipple Hill [p. 54], and Lexington's Great Meadow [p. 56].

Myth: the Minuteman is packed with bikers, in-line skaters, children, dogs, corporate strollers and loiterers.
Fact: okay, it's mobbed, but go on a weekday.

Facilities:
Water and facilities are available in businesses along Mass Ave in Arlington and at Lexington Center. At the time of publication, portable toilets were sited at the trail's end in Bedford. Water is located near the Arlington Reservoir at Hurd Field.

Map II: The Northeastern Suburbs

19.6 miles

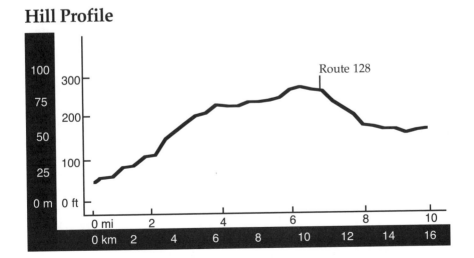

BEDFORD

225

4

128

Parker
Meadow

Great
Meadow

Arlington
Reservoir

Track

60

Revere St

Maple St

LEXINGTON

Massachusetts Ave

Spy
Pond

S

16

ARLINGTON

Varnum St

2

Alewife T

Hill Profile

Route 128

100
75
50
25
0 m

300
200
100
0 ft

0 mi   2   4   6   8   10
0 km   2   4   6   8   10   12   14   16

53

Whipple Hill

Distances:	**Total Miles**	**3.8**
	Arlington Reservoir Loop	1.4

Surfaces: Trail and side of road.

Directions:
1. Start at parking turn-out off Winchester Dr.
2. Run east to a pond, bear left onto a trail around the pond.
3. As you descend the hill, avoid branching left onto any of several footpaths that lead out of the forest. The trail bends right along a stone wall, and then continues down.
4. After crossing a stream, turn left and follow the trail to the exit at Summer St.
5. Cross Summer St to Haskell St (slightly to the left).
6. Follow Haskell St to Lowell St and turn left.
7. Turn right and complete a loop around the Reservoir.
8. Retrace the path to the forest and take the central trail up Whipple Hill. Turn left at the pond and then left again at a smaller (seasonal) pond. Hike the rocky trail to the summit, and then descend back to the start.

Notes: At 374 feet, Whipple Hill offers a panoramic view. For a smoother (but equally steep) ascent or descent, try the combination of Whipple and Russell roads. As the map suggests, this run can be combined with the Minuteman Trail [p. 52] and Lexington's Great Meadow [see p. 57 for detail]. For additional hills, detour up Westmoreland Ave, circle through the Mt. Gilboa conservation area, and rejoin the route via Madison or Crescent Hill Avenues.

Facilities: In summer, restrooms are available at Arlington Reservoir's beach. Water is located next to the Minuteman Trail at Hurd Field.

3.8 miles

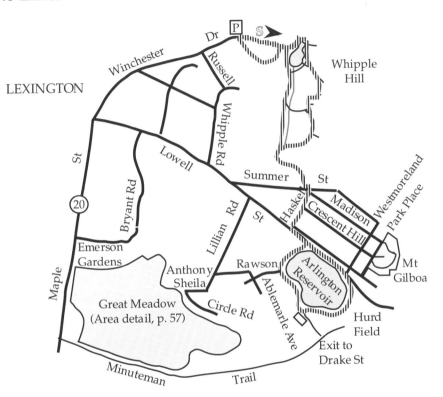

Hill Profile

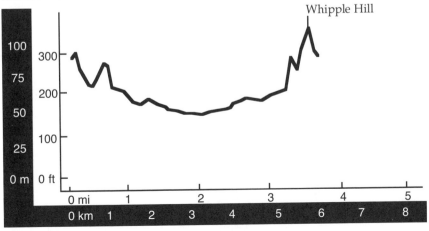

Lexington Meadow

Area: Approximately one hundred and fifty acres.

Surfaces: Soft dirt are trails concentrated on the perimeter. Seasonal swampiness renders the Meadow's interior inhospitable and ecologically sensitive. Please tread lightly.

Directions: In addition to the network of trails shown on the map, runners may wish to explore the Whipple Hill run (3.8 miles) and the Arlington Reservoir Loop (1.4 miles).

<u>To Whipple Hill:</u>

Exit Great Meadow onto Emerson Gardens Rd. Turn right and continue to Bryant Rd. Follow Bryant to end and turn right on Lowell. Refer to p. 54 for step-by-step directions.

<u>To Arlington Reservoir:</u>

Exit at Sheila Rd. Turn left onto Lillian Rd. Turn right onto Anthony Rd. Turn right onto Albermarle Ave. Turn left onto Rawson and continue straight to the Reservoir.

Notes: Lexington's Great Meadow, like the Great Meadows at Concord [p. 90] and Weir Hill [p. 98], surpasses our expectations for an ordinary meadow. Some key ingredient makes this ordinary meadow "Great." Some temptation lures the ducks out or their migratory routes. Some nutrient-rich life-force pushes oak, beech and birch trees out of soupy soil. Some secret rumination awaits the runner who succeeds in getting lost on these densely knotted trails. Some screwy great thing. Of course, a swamp really isn't a great place to run, but it's an extraordinary place to try.

Map II: The Northeastern Suburbs

Area Detail

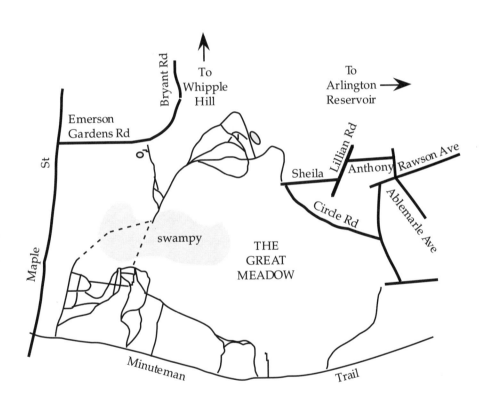

LEXINGTON

See pp. 52-55 for context.

Four Corners

Arlington-Winchester-Woburn-Lexington

Distances:	**Total Miles**	**8.0**

Surfaces: Sidewalk and side of road.

Directions:
1. Start from where Lowell St branches off Mass Ave.
2. Turn right onto Park Ave.
3. Continue across Summer St onto Park Ave Extension.
4. Bear left onto Forest St.
5. [Hill option: turn right onto Dodge and run up to Turkey Hill Reservation and back].
6. Turn left onto Ridge St.
7. Ridge St becomes Waltham St.
8. Turn left onto Lexington St.
9. Turn left onto Lowell St.
10. Turn right onto Maple St.
11. Turn right onto Mass Ave and return to the start.

Notes: Even if you dodge Dodge St, there are plenty of ups and downs ahead. One scrap of consolation: the course undulates around (not over) Whipple Hill [p. 54] which, at 374 feet, peaks higher than any other point in the Boston metropolitan area. If you're aching for a difficult long run, combine this run with the Mystic Lakes Loop by following Hutchinson Rd eastward.

Facilities: Rest rooms and water are available at businesses along Mass Ave and near the corner of Lexington and Lowell Streets.

Map II: The Northeastern Suburbs

8.0 miles

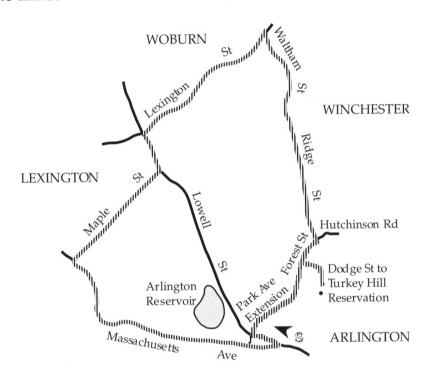

Hill Profile

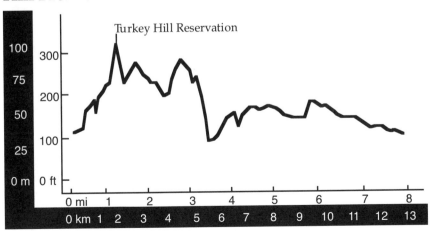

Turkey Hill Reservation

Mystic Lakes

Distances:	**Total Miles**	**5.0**
	Using Hill Loop	5.2

Surfaces: Paved pathway, sidewalk, and dirt trail.

Directions:
1. Start at the Sandy Neck Beach parking area.
2. Run south along Mystic Valley Parkway.
3. Turn right onto High Street.
4. Turn right onto Mystic Valley Parkway (which continues westbound on the opposite side of the bridge).
5. Turn right onto Mystic St.
6. [Hill Option: bear left on Ridge St; turn right on Winchester Road; turn left on Old Mystic St].
7. Turn right onto Everett Ave.
8. Turn right onto Bacon St.
9. Turn right onto Lakeview Rd.
10. Turn right onto Mystic Valley Parkway.

Notes: East beats West on the scenic-ometer. On the eastern side, you can run near the water's edge and explore trails whereas on the western side, the views are obstructed by houses. Still, if you're due for some hill work, the west side has some of the stoutest grades around. Try the hill option, or head up one of the left turns off Mystic St. Add an additional two miles to the loop by running south along the Mystic Valley River.

Facilities: Restrooms and water are available at the beach house near the start and inside the Community Safety (Police) Building on Mystic St just south of the suggested route.

5.0 miles

Hill Profile

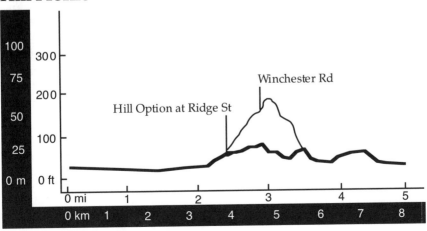

Somerville

Distances:	**Total Miles**	**6.8**
	Mystic River Reservation Loop	2.5

Surfaces: Sidewalk, side of road, and stairways.

Directions:

1. Warm up prior to start at Somerville Ave and Lowell St.
2. Shuffle up Lowell St and turn right onto Summer St.
3. Descend into town and turn left onto Stone Ave.
4. Continue up through Prospect Hill Park using the stairs.
5. Turn left onto Munroe St then right onto Walnut St.
6. Turn left onto Broadway and run over Winter Hill.
7. At Powder House Square, turn right onto College Ave.
8. Near the top of the hill, turn left up the Tufts stairs.
9. Follow a paved pathway to Packard Ave and turn right.
10. Packard Ave bends left and becomes Capen St (East).
11. Turn left onto Winthrop and left onto Powder Hse Blvd.
12. Follow College Ave down through Davis Square and follow Elm St back to the start.

Notes: From the idyllic Tufts campus to the gritty Somerville sidewalks, nobody here is afraid of gut-busting hills. However, as a safety precaution, solo and night runners should switch to the popular Thursday night runs sponsored by the Somerville Road Runners and Khoury's Spa on Broadway. For additional miles (and flat terrain) run north to the Mystic River Reservation. This two-and-a-half mile loop of paved pathways is remarkably scenic given that its three borders are busy highways.

Facilities: Water is available at the Central Hill Playground (near Highland Ave and Walnut St) and at Powder House Sq. Restrooms are available at the Davis Sq MBTA station.

Map II: The Northeastern Suburbs

6.8 miles

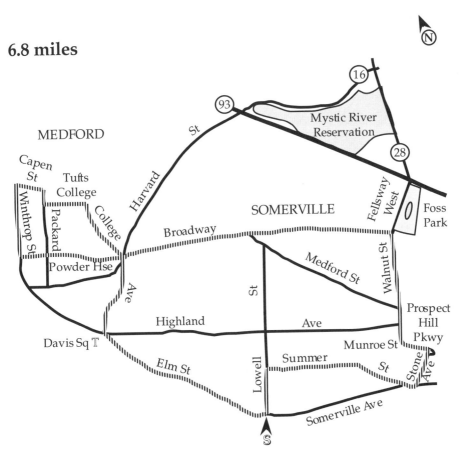

Hill Profile

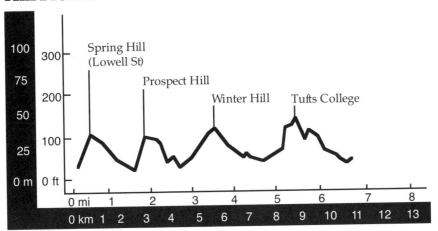

Middlesex Fells-South

| Distances: | **Total Miles** | 2.8 |

Surfaces: Fire roads (dirt and gravel).

Directions:
1. Start at the Bellevue Pond parking area.
2. Run west on South Border Rd to the fire road entrance.
3. Enter the Reservation and follow Middle Road to the edge of South Reservoir.
4. Return on East Dam Rd, Red Cross Path, and Mud Rd.
5. For a great view of the city, climb to Wright's Tower.
6. Lap Bellevue Pond to cool down.

Notes: Of all the great places to explore in the Reservation, why this loop? Why indeed, when there is so much to discover, but before setting off on your own adventure, consider the following tips:

◇ Consult the trail map posted at the parking area.
◇ If you're hoping to run, stick to the fire roads. The color-coded trails may appear run-able, but they are better suited for hiking punctuated by mild boulder scrambling.
◇ Access is prohibited to the areas immediately surrounding the reservoirs.
◇ Over 150 plant species have disappeared from the park over the past century. Please don't trample.

Some runners choose to run around the periphery of the Reservation rather than within it. The Spot Pond run [p. 66] is popular, as are runs that incorporate South Border Rd.

Facilities: Neither restrooms nor water is available.

5.0 miles

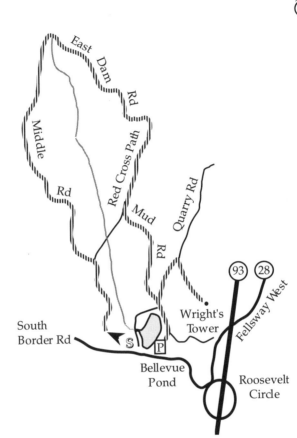

MEDFORD

Middlesex Fells
Reservation

Hill Profile

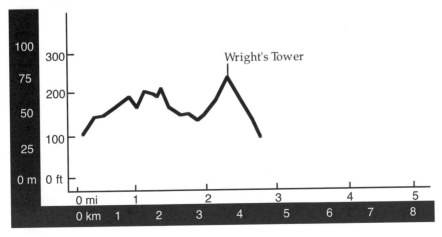

Spot Pond-Middlesex Fells

Distances:

Total Miles	**5.0**
Using Bear Hill Loop	6.0

Surfaces: Sidewalk and side of the road. Trail optional.

Directions:

1. Start at the Sheepfold parking area.
2. Return to main road and turn left onto Fellsway West.
3. Turn right onto Lover's Lane (leading to South St).
4. Continue on Pond St, Woodland Rd and Elm St.
5. Return to start via Fellsway West.

Notes: Watch out for fast-moving traffic on Fellsway West which parallels the freeway. For a more scenic (and difficult) run, start inside Middlesex Fells Reservation with the Bear Hill Loop:

1. Head north out of the end of Sheepfold parking area.
2. Run to the bottom of the Soap Box Derby Track.
3. Turn right (east) and continue past the white trail to the next fire road (Bear Hill Rd).
4. Turn left on Bear Hill Rd and continue uphill to Bear Hill Tower.
5. Retrace your steps back downhill and turn right to descend the north slope to Bear Hill parking area.
6. Cross under the freeway to North Border Rd and continue to the intersection of Main St and South St.
7. Rejoin the Spot Pond Loop.

Facilities: Restrooms and water are available at the Reservation Headquarters (at Pond St and Woodland Rd), and at Flynn Rink near the Highland Ave rotary.

5.0 miles

North Border Rd

South St

STONEHAM

Bear Hill Rd

Pond St

Soap Box Derby Track

Spot Pond

Reservation HQ

S

P

Woodland

Middlesex Fells
Reservation

Fellsway West

28

93

Wright's
Pond

Rd

Highland Ave

St

Elm

Hill Profile

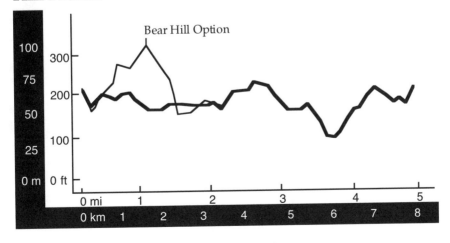

Bear Hill Option

100	300
75	200
50	100
25	
0 m	0 ft

0 mi   1   2   3   4   5

0 km   1   2   3   4   5   6   7   8

Melrose

Distances:	**Total Miles**	8.3

Surfaces: Paved and dirt pathways, sidewalk and side of road.

Directions:
1. Start at the Pine Banks Park parking area.
2. Loop around Pine Banks: start up Island Pond Rd, bear right onto Summit Rd (unpaved), continue across Banks Rd onto a trail. The trail follows an embankment and then makes a hairpin right turn back toward the parking area.
3. Turn left (out of the Pine Banks entrance) onto Main St.
4. Turn left onto Leonard St, and as you approach the top of the hill, turn right into Waitts Mount Park.
5. Loop around the Park and continue to end of Leonard St.
6. Turn right onto Tremont St.
7. Turn left onto Mountain Ave.
8. Turn left onto Mt. Vernon St which winds up to Forest St.
9. Turn right onto Forest St
10. Turn left onto Lebanon St.
11. Merge right onto Main St; turn left onto Crystal St.
12. Complete a sharp left turn onto Lynn Fells Pkwy (and continue on the road or through Ell Pond Park).
13. Turn left onto Wyoming Ave; turn right onto Brown St.
14. Turn left onto Mt. Vernon St; turn left to reach Boston Rock Rd, then turn left again and loop around hill.
15. Turn left onto Mt Vernon Ave. Cross Sylvan St and the playing fields to return to the Pine Banks Parking area.

Notes: A decent route through commercial and recreational areas with a variety of surfaces and two very steep hills.

Facilities: Restrooms and water are available in businesses on Main St and Wyoming Ave.

8.3 miles

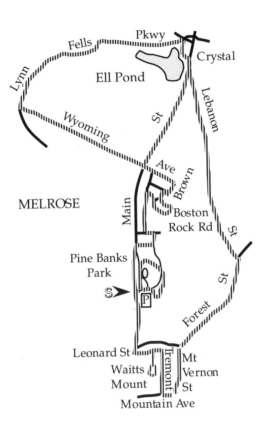

Hill Profile

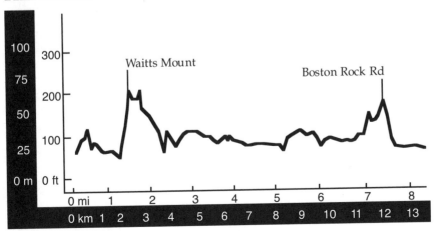

Lake Quannapowitt

Distances:

Total Miles	**5.6**
Lake Quannapowitt Loop	3.3
Prospect St Loop	2.3

Surfaces: Dirt and paved pathways, sidewalk, and side of road.

Directions:
1. Start at the parking area adjacent to Veteran's Field.
2. Follow the paved pathway to Lakeside Ave.
3. Turn left onto Lakeside Ave.
4. Turn right onto North Ave.
5. Turn right onto Quannapowitt and follow a dirt trail around the top of the lake.
6. Turn right onto Main St. Continue around the lake and turn left onto Lake St.
7. Turn right onto Church St and rejoin the dirt path which leads to Veteran's Field.
8. Cross the intersection and tracks safely. Continue uphill on Prospect St.
9. Turn left onto Park Ave.
10. Turn left onto Bellevue Rd.
11. Turn left onto Converse St and descend a steep grade.
12. Converse St becomes Gould St. Continue on Gould St.
13. Turn left onto Emerson St to return to the start.

Notes: Lake Quannapowitt serves as a home base for Wakefield runners. It's comfortable and safe, but you can't stay there forever. Runners who migrate out from the lake will find more rigorous loops. For a hillbilly's heaping helping of topographic relief, try Prospect and Converse Streets. Be sure not to over-extend your stride as you descend Converse.

Facilities: A gas station is located at North Ave and Church St.

Map II: The Northeastern Suburbs

5.6 miles

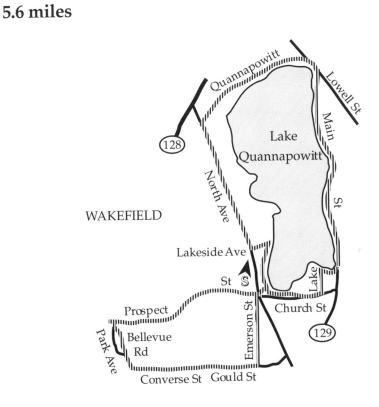

Hill Profile

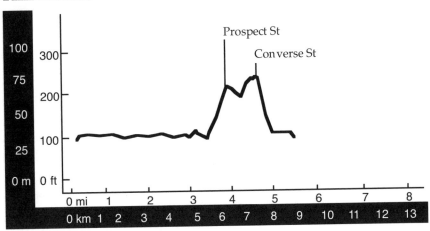

Breakheart Reservation

Distances:	**Total Miles**	2.9

Surfaces: Road and paved pathway.

Directions:

1. To reach Breakheart by car, take Route 1, exit at Lynn Fells Pkwy (south) and turn right onto Forest St.
2. The run begins at the Park Headquarters.
3. Follow Pine Tops Rd counter-clockwise.
4. At Pearce Beach, turn left onto Elm Rd.
5. Turn left onto Hemlock Rd.
6. Turn right to rejoin Pine Tops Rd.
7. Return to the start.

Notes:

The suggested route undulates at first and then swells to impressive crests and troughs. Should the in-line skaters loose control on sharp descents, it's nice to know you can ditch them by jumping off the pavement onto any of several well-maintained trails. You can circle the lakes (Pearce and Silver Lake Trails) follow the river (Saugus River Trail) or take to the hills (Fox Run Trail, Ridge Trail, Breakheart Hill Trail).

Facilities:

Restrooms and water are available at Pearce Beach and Kasabuski Rink. Water is available at Park Headquarters.

Map II: The Northeastern Suburbs

2.9 miles

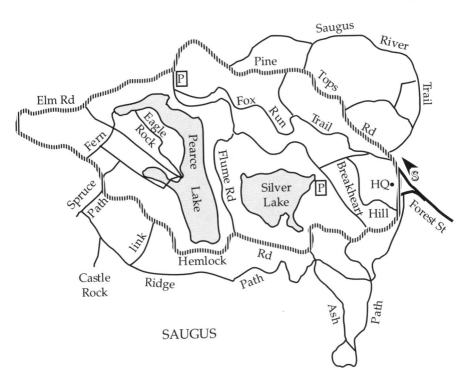

Hill Profile

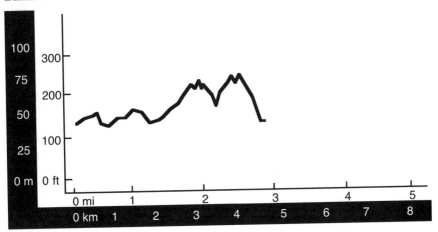

Lynn Woods Reservation

Distances:

Total Miles	**4.9**
Mt. Gilead Loop	0.6
Dungeon Rd	1.0

Surfaces: Unpaved roads and dirt trails with some rocks.

Directions:

1. Start from the Great Woods Rd parking area.
2. Enter forest on Great Woods Rd.
3. Hill Option: turn left onto Loop Rd. Climb Mt. Gilead to the Steel Tower and descend.
4. Turn right onto Dungeon Rd to return to Great Woods Rd.
5. Great Woods Rd bends left and becomes Penny Brook Rd.
6. Turn left onto Waycross Rd. Continue to Breeds Pond where the road bends north and turns into Dungeon Rd. (The rocky steps to Dungeon Rock may be used, but the terrain is better suited for hiking than running).
7. Turn right onto Cooke Rd.
8. Climb Burrill Hill to the Stone Tower and descend.
9. Turn right onto Great Woods Rd and return to the start.

Notes: Consider the hill option mandatory. Mt. Gilead adds a degree of difficulty and an excellent view. The "truly optional" label applies to the many side footpaths as well as the major trails north and west of Walden Pond. Although it is possible to forge an awkward loop around Walden Pond, the trails at the far (northwestern) end of the pond are at best unpleasant and at worst impassable.

Facilities: Water is available at the Park Dept. on Penny Brook Rd.

4.9 miles

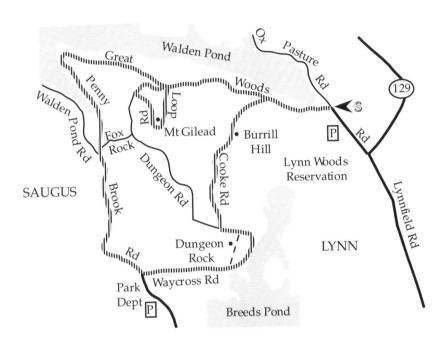

Hill Profile

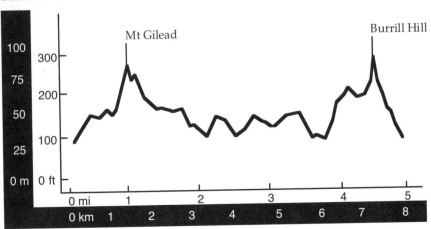

Nahant

Distances:	**Total Miles**	**8.6**
	Little Nahant Loop	1.1
	Big Nahant Loop	4.2

Surfaces: Paved pathway and side of road.

Directions:
1. Start from Ward Bath House and run south alongside Nahant Beach Parkway.
2. Turn left onto Wilson Rd. Wilson Rd turns into Little Nahant Rd, which bends back to the main road.
3. Turn left onto Nahant Rd.
4. Turn right onto Vernon St, and loop back to Cliff St.
5. Turn left onto Cliff St. Cliff St bends right to become Willow Rd. Follow Willow Rd around Nahant Harbor to the golf course where the road ends. Bear left onto a gravel path which leads through the park at Bailey's Hill.
6. Pass through the park; turn right onto Trimountain Rd.
7. Turn left onto Gardiner Rd. Bear right onto Castle Rd.
8. Rejoin Nahant Rd and turn left to return to the start.

Notes: A lone runner sets out for Nahant. A stew of salty smells surfs over the sandy flats and rolling hills. A winter wind whips the waves. A pair of bare legs propels the runner along the rocks at the edge of a harbor. A freshly painted house stands out of the fog like the crisp white sails in the bay. The wind shifts as the New England runner swings around and paces homeward across an isolated strip of land.

Facilities: The Ward Bath House hours are 8-11 A.M. Water fountains are located at the start and alongside Nahant Rd.

Map II: The Northeastern Suburbs

8.6 miles

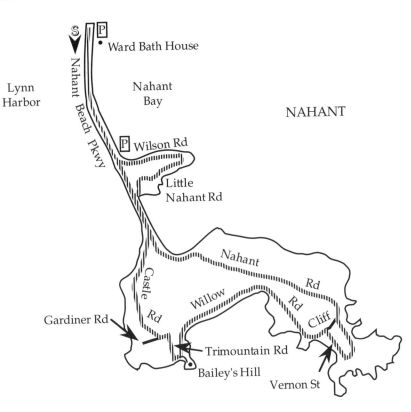

NAHANT

Lynn Harbor

Nahant Bay

Nahant Beach Pkwy

Ward Bath House

Wilson Rd

Little Nahant Rd

Nahant Rd

Castle Rd

Willow Rd

Cliff Rd

Gardiner Rd

Trimountain Rd

Bailey's Hill

Vernon St

Hill Profile

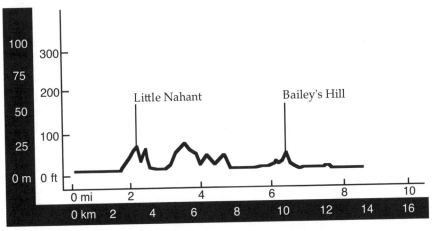

Little Nahant

Bailey's Hill

Weston Reservoir

Map III: The Northwestern Suburbs

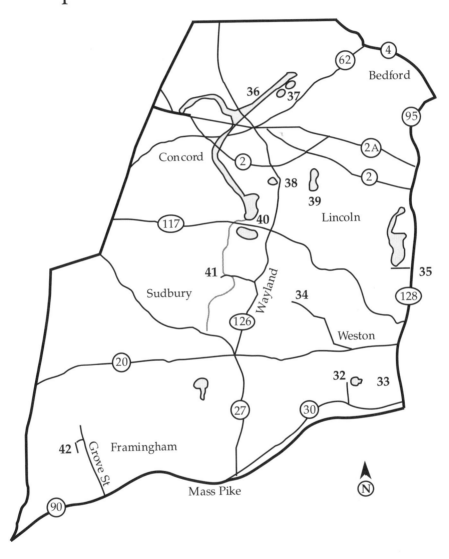

Let me live where I will, on this side is the city, on that the wilderness, and ever I am leaving the city more and more, and withdrawing into the wilderness.

- Henry David Thoreau

Weston Reservoir

Distances:	**Total Miles**	**2.5**
	Reservoir Loop	2.0
	Canal Loop	0.6
	Combined with Doublet Hill [p. 82]	5.6

Surfaces: Trail.

Directions:

1. Turn off Route 30 onto Ash St.
2. Start at Ash St parking area.
3. Follow the trail around the Reservoir.
4. Loop around the Canal and return to the start.
5. [Hill Option: follow the Aqueduct for 0.2 miles; turn left onto Newton St.; turn right onto Doublet Hill Rd and follow the map for the Doublet Hill run].

Notes:

Although mapmakers place the Weston Reservoir within a mile of the busy Turnpike interchange, this area has the feel of remote wilderness. As you set off around the water or explore the basin's gentle slopes, the murmur of traffic fades until all you hear is the squish of leaves and pine needles under your shoes. Stay alert for the occasional rocks and roots. For additional miles, sniff out a trail near the parking area that departs west from Ash St. Follow this trail west and cross Wellesley St to hook up with the vast network of trails surrounding Regis College.

Facilities: Neither restrooms nor water is available.

Map III: The Northwestern Suburbs

2.5 miles

WESTON

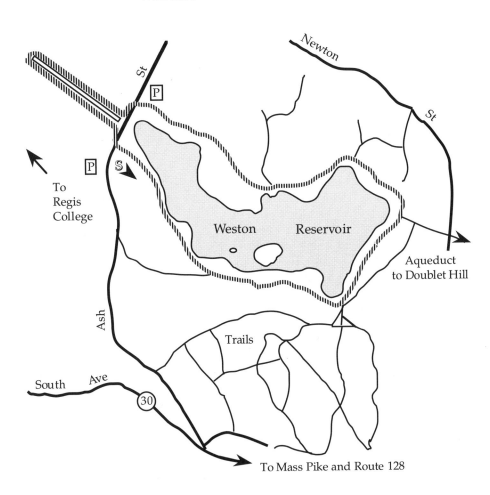

Doublet Hill

Distances:	**Total Miles**	**3.0**
	Doublet Hill Loop	1.7
	Newton St to Trailhead (out & back)	1.4
	Combined with Weston Reservoir [p. 80]	5.6

Surfaces: Trail.

Directions: 1. Start from the Aqueduct at Newton St. [Parking is discouraged on the private roads surrounding Doublet Hill, so if you're arriving by car, the most convenient place to park is Weston Reservoir].
2. Caution: watch and listen for cars coming around the bend when turning onto Newton St.
3. Turn right onto Doublet Hill Rd.
4. The trailhead starts at the top of Doublet Hill Rd.
5. Follow the map's suggested route to descend the hill, explore the low-lying pond and forest, and return uphill to a spectacular view.

Notes: If you've run the entire route, the view at the end is sure to be breathtaking. Wander the trails, or--if you prefer a more stable surface--try running along the Aqueduct. Note that some of the trails outside the public shaded areas on the map cross private land. Although recent years have witnessed an increase in development and mountain biking, much of the area remains unspoiled. Please tread lightly.

Facilities: Neither restrooms or water is available.

3.1 miles

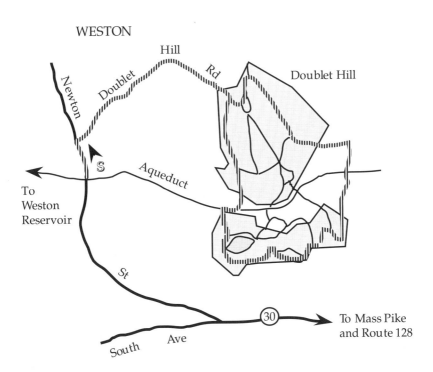

Hill Profile

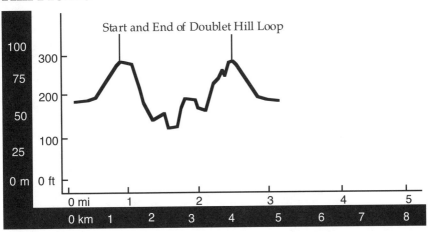

Cherry Brook

Distances:	**Total Miles**	5.7
	North of Concord Rd	1.7
	South of Concord Rd	4.0

Surfaces: Trail.

Directions: To reach the Conservation Area from Weston Center, follow Concord Rd north. Bear left at the fork (as opposed to right onto Merriam St). Turn right at the wood sign marking the entrance.

Either follow the suggested route which starts from the parking area and playing fields, or explore the numerous trails. As a navigational aide, certain trail markers bear letters or numbers that correspond to those on the map.

Notes: North of Concord Rd, the countryside is a portrait of productive civic harmony. Upon breaking out of the woods you might encounter an orchard, a garden plot, a pile of compost, the edge of an old quarry, a hint of burning brush.

South of Concord Rd, one of the few echoes of this industriousness is the abandoned railroad, where nature has done its best to reclaim the marginal trail alongside the tracks. To avoid possible injury, never run on the actual tracks (abandoned or otherwise)! If you prefer broad trails, there are many open paths through the woods. The topography is mostly flat with dips and bumps rarely exceeding twenty feet.

Facilities: Neither restrooms nor water is available.

Map III: The Northwestern Suburbs

5.7 miles

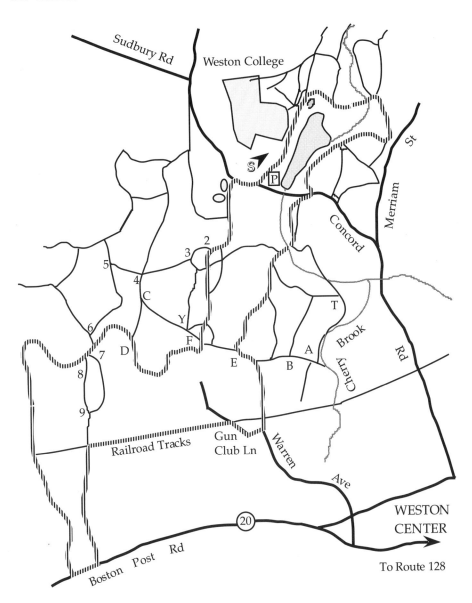

Hobbs Brook Basin (Cambridge Reservoir)

Distances:	**Total Miles**	**6.0**
	Including Prospect Hill (out & back)	8.4

Surfaces: Side of road.

Directions:
1. Start at Prospect Hill Park.
2. Turn left out of parking area onto Totten Pond Rd.
3. Cross to right side of street and continue across overpass onto Winter St. Continue around Basin on Winter St.
4. Turn right onto Old County Rd.
5. Turn right onto Trapelo Rd.
6. Turn right onto Smith St which turns into Wyman St.
7. Turn left onto Totten Pond Rd and return to start.
8. [Hill Option: climb and descend Prospect Hill Rd].

Notes: Run cautiously along Totten Pond Rd, and try to avoid running in this commercial area during commute hours. Hobbs is worth visiting even if you're not one of the white-collar faithful. In fact, several suburbanites stray out of neighboring Lincoln and Weston to make Hobbs part of their weekend long-runs. Prospect Hill is too steep to include as part of an effective training program, but if you're in the mood for physical punishment and spiritual reward, then go take in the views from the top.

Facilities: Restrooms are available at gas stations on Trapelo Rd and Smith St.

6.0 miles

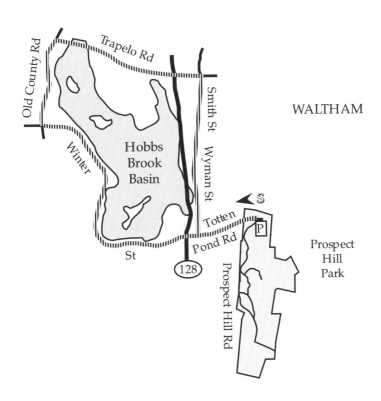

Hill Profile

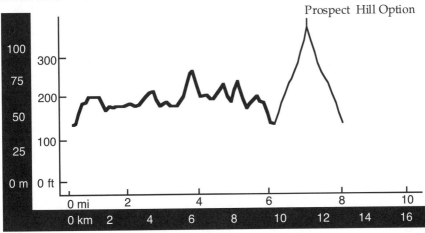

North Concord

Distances: **Total Miles**   **7.1**
                Estabrook Trail Loop   3.6
                Merged Loops   10.4

Surfaces: Side of road, paved pathway and trails (optional).

Directions: 1. Start north of Concord Center at North Bridge Parking.
                2. Run north on Monument and turn left onto Liberty St.
                3. Turn right onto Estabrook Rd.
                4. Bear left onto Barnes Hill Rd; cross Lowell Rd and continue on Barrett's Mill Rd.
                5. Bear right onto College Rd.
                6. Turn left onto Annursnac Hill Rd. Follow loop around hill and descend on Annursnac Hill Rd.
                7. Turn right onto Strawberry Hill Rd.
                8. Retrace path and turn right onto Lowell Rd.
                9. Turn left onto Liberty St and retrace the path to the start.

Notes: At the start, visit North Bridge Battle Ground and the Minute Man Statue. If you choose the trail option, follow Estabrook Rd to the end of the pavement and continue almost a mile farther on the trail. Shortly after passing a stone marker, turn left onto Hugh Cargill Rd (marked by a red blaze). For additional miles, combine this run with Great Meadows Concord Unit [p. 90] by following either Great Meadows Rd or the abandoned railroad bed.

                For an informal group run, join the Concord Runners each Saturday at 8 A.M. in front of the Colonial Inn at Concord Center. Also, explore the vast trail networks of Carlisle north of Concord.

Facilities: Restrooms are available at the Visitor's Center on Liberty.

Map III: The Northwestern Suburbs

7.1 miles

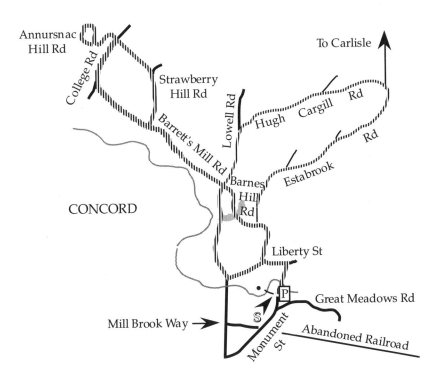

Hill Profile

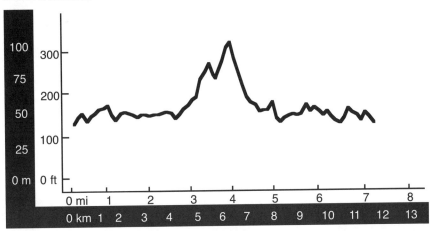

Great Meadows-Concord Unit

Distances:	**Total Miles**	3.6
	Dike Trail (around Lower Pond)	1.7

Surfaces: Trail.

Directions: 1. Start at the Great Meadows National Wildlife Refuge parking area off Monsen Rd.
2. Begin running counter-clockwise on Dike Trail.
3. Continue along the northern edge of the Refuge until the grassy trail becomes a narrow asphalt road (Great Meadows Rd).
4. Merge with Monument St.
5. Turn left onto abandoned railroad bed. [Note that the path eventually dips to the right of the railroad bed].
6. Follow the path across a field, a road and down an embankment before rejoining the railroad bed and returning to the start.

Notes: Great Meadow's Concord Unit provides excellent habitat for migratory runners; they drop in from miles around to enjoy the soft surfaces and swampy serenity. For a longer loop, runners may wish to follow Monument St to Bedford St and return by cutting diagonally through Sleepy Hollow Cemetery, past a small pond, through a patch of woods, and along two sides of a field.

Facilities: Restrooms are adjacent to the parking area.

Map III: The Northwestern Suburbs

3.6 miles

CONCORD

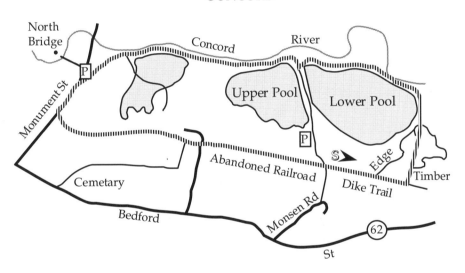

Walden Pond

Distances:	**Total Miles**	**4.3**
	Walden Pond Path loop	1.7
	Hapgood Town Forest loop	1.0

Surfaces: Trail and side of road.

Directions:

1. Start at Walden Pond State Reservation parking area.
2. Cross Walden St and complete Pond Path loop.
3. Turn left onto trail alongside Walden St.
4. Shortly after crossing Route 2, turn right into the southwestern entrance to Hapgood Town Forest.
5. Circle around Fairyland Pond as indicated on the map and return on Walden St.
6. After re-crossing Route 2, turn right onto Boundary Rd.
7. Bear left onto Bean Field Rd, then left again down to the Thoreau House site.
8. Turn left onto Wyman Rd, then right onto Woods Path.
9. From Woods Path, turn left onto Ridge Path and return along the rim of the kettle.

Notes: Detailed directions wouldn't have pleased Thoreau, and if you follow these, you might hear his chuckling on the breeze: "Conformity! Simplify!"

If the spirit moves you to wander aimlessly, you might lose yourself on Pine Hill, or run up against Emerson's Cliff, or stumble into Heywood's Meadow. To assist you in getting lost, I have omitted these areas from this map.

Facilities: Restrooms and water are available at Reservation HQ.

4.3 miles

CONCORD

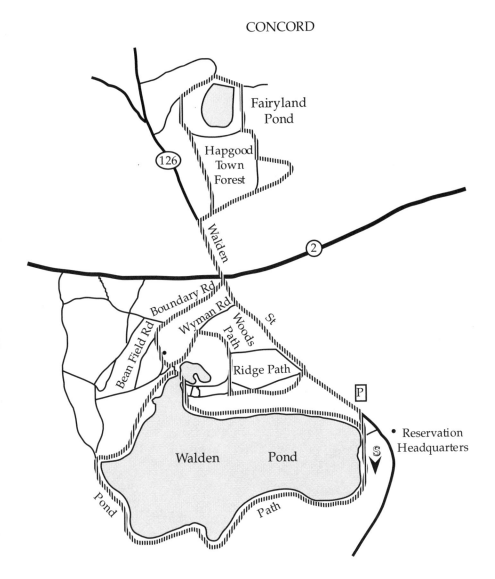

Fairyland
Pond

Hapgood
Town
Forest

126

Walden

2

Boundary Rd

Bean Field Rd

Wyman Rd

Woods
Path

St

Ridge Path

P

Reservation
Headquarters

S

Walden   Pond

Pond

Path

LINCOLN

Sandy Pond

Distances:	**Total Miles**	**4.9**

Surfaces: Trail, with rocks and roots dominating the western shore.

Directions:

1. Start at Lincoln Schools off Lincoln Rd.
2. Run west out of the western parking area.
3. Turn right onto pipeline; turn right again behind the schools; turn left through field.
4. Turn left onto Sandy Pond Rd.
5. Turn left onto the trail opposite the pumping station. Follow the trail over the hill and turn right to return to Sandy Pond Rd. Continue up the road to the path around the pond. [Note that the first half mile is very rocky. To avoid scrambling in places, join the pond loop farther up].
6. Merge right onto "Bike Trail" at intersection.
7. Turn right at marker 24 onto Black Gum Trail.
8. Turn right at marker 27.
9. Turn right onto Cedar Hill Loop. Follow this loop to its end and turn right. Follow trail along water, and then branch uphill toward DeCordova museum.
10. Skirt left of the museum and follow trail downhill.
11. Turn right onto Sandy Pond Rd and retrace the path across the field back to the start.

Notes: Explore! A few trails lead westward over Pine Hill to Goose and Walden Ponds [p. 92]. Another network of paths extends eastward to Lincoln Reservoir and beyond. You will also discover trails south and west of Lincoln Schools. For example, by turning left at the pipeline, a runner may follow the Three Friends, Stonewall, and Hemlock trails to Route 126 and return on Baker Bridge Rd.

Facilities: Water is available on the schools' central athletic field.

4.9 miles

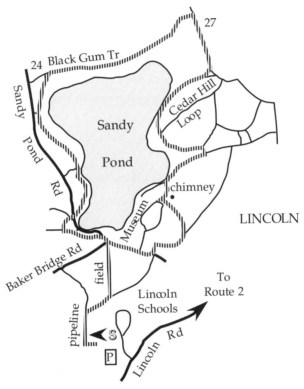

Hill Profile

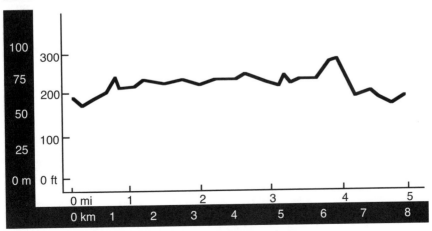

Mt. Misery

Distances: **Total Miles** 5.1

Surfaces: Trail and paved pathway.

Directions:
1. Start at Mt. Misery parking area off Route 117 in South Lincoln.
2. Hike up and to the left briefly to warm up.
3. Begin running over the first hill, then bear left on Kettle Trail; turn right at marker "3" and continue along water.
4. Continue on Kettle Trail to the "F,9" marker.
5. Turn right (onto "F") and continue downhill; branch left onto Wolf Pine Trail and hook back uphill (across "E" to "G") and ascend Mt. Misery.
6. Continue downhill and turn right back onto Kettle Trail.
7. Turn right and follow Beech Tree Trail to St. Anne's.
8. Cross Route 126 to a paved pathway and turn right.
9. Continue across 117, past Winchelsea lane, and after a short hill, look for trail marker at right (adjacent to #234).
10. Follow trail around Farrar Pond. At the western end, stones allow for a cautious crossing between pond and river.
11. Trail 1, which passes along the fence line between two private residences, allows the public a quiet return to 117.
12. Trail 2 starts from the canoe launch parking area and runs alongside 117 to the start.

Notes: Woods, hills, swamps, fields, streams, ponds, mossy trails, rivers, and coves. Explore northward to discover excellent running connections to the Fairhaven Bay and Walden Pond areas [p. 92].

Facilities: Neither restrooms nor water is available.

Map III: The Northwestern Suburbs

5.1 miles

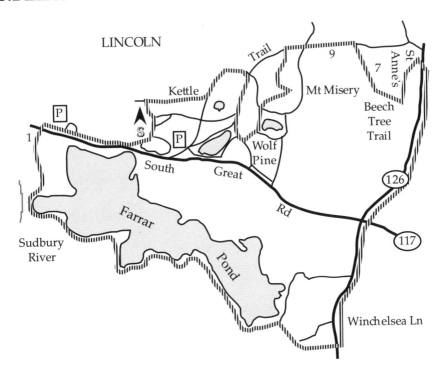

Hill Profile

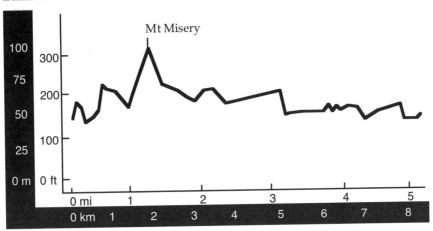

Sudbury River

| Distances: | **Total Miles** | **13.5** |
| | Weir Hill Loop | 1.0 |

Surfaces: Trail, paved pathway, and side of road.

Directions:
1. Start at the Great Meadows National Wildlife Refuge (Weir Hill Area) Visitor's Center.
2. Begin running counter-clockwise on the hiking trail.
3. Turn right where the pathway intersects the road, and turn left onto Weir Hill Rd.
4. Turn right onto Sherman's Bridge Road.
5. Turn left onto Water Row; continue on River Rd.
6. Merge right onto Rte 20, then turn left onto Landham Rd.
7. Turn left onto Pelham Island Rd and skirt Heard Pond.
8. Rejoin Rte 20 briefly, then turn left onto Rte 27.
9. Turn right onto Glezen Lane; then bear left onto Moore Rd.
10. Turn left onto Concord Rd.
11. Turn left onto Sherman's Bridge Rd.
12. Turn right onto Weir Hill Rd and right again towards Visitor's Center. Turn right onto the hiking trail and run past a shelter and a pond to complete the Weir Hill loop.

Notes: Although this route starts with Weir hill, the next several miles are flat, and there is little to distract runners from their swampy contemplation of the landscape. Still, the muscle groups that slacked off on Water Row must come to attention for the rolling terrain through Wayland.

Facilities: Restrooms and water are available at the Visitor's Center.

Map III: The Northwestern Suburbs

13.5 miles

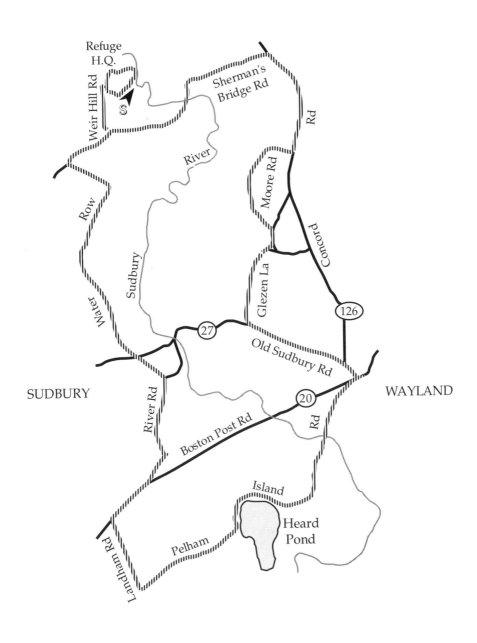

Callahan State Forest

Distances:	**Total Miles**	**8.2**

Surfaces: Dirt roads, trails, and side of road.

Directions:

1. Start at the Millwood St entrance to Callahan Forest.
2. Run north and bear right onto Packard Trail.
3. Turn left onto Pipeline Trail and continue over the hill.
4. Use caution as you leave the woods and turn left onto Edmands Rd. Continue on Edmands Rd to the Framingham-Southborough Town Line and turn right to rejoin trails.
5. Cross a meadow and begin Pine Tree Loop around Beebe Pond. Before completing the loop around the pond, continue straight onto Bear Paw Trail.
6. Cross the power line corridor and continue to a dirt road.
7. Turn left onto Broad Meadow Rd.
8. Turn left on Parmenter Rd and run past Eastleigh Farm.
9. At 1037 Edmands Rd, turn right onto Red Tail Trail.
10. Return to the start via Rocky Rd, Pinecone, Coco, and Earthen Dam trails.

Notes: No, Framingham is not all mega-malls and cineplexes. Northwestern Framingham surpasses all expectations. If you're willing to share narrow, hilly roads with backcountry drivers, then fashion loops using Belknap, Millwood, Winch, Grove, Edmands, Nixon, Parmenter and Wayside. If, however, you prefer peaceful trails, then explore the State Forest. Although a pessimist might focus on the swamps, mosquitoes, thick vegetation and rocks, an optimist will enjoy the ponds, fireflies, wildflowers, and the challenging scramble up Mt. Gibbs.

Facilities: None. Private farms sell fruit and beverages seasonally.

8.2 miles

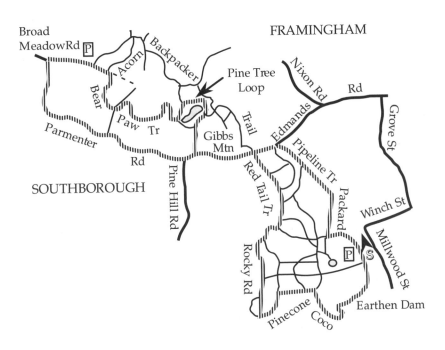

Hill Profile

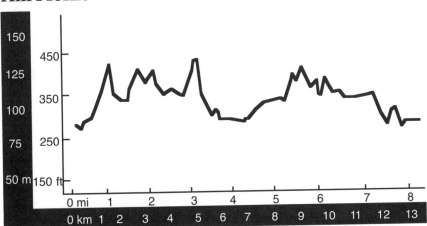

Maugus Hill, Wellesley

Map IV: The Southwestern Suburbs

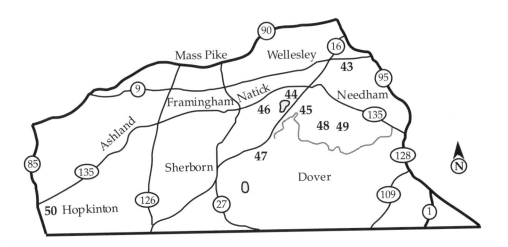

A plan calls for the most active imagination. It calls for the most severe discipline also. The plan is what determines everything; it is the decisive moment.

- LeCorbusier

Wellesley Town Forest

Distances:	**Total Miles**	**3.9**
	Town Forest Loop	1.9
	Centennial Park Loop	1.3

Surfaces: Trail and side of road.

Directions:
1. Start at the Longfellow Pond Parking area.
2. Run clockwise to the opposite side of the pond.
3. At marker #4, follow the center trail up a ridge.
4. Continue over the hill and descend to Oakland St.
5. Turn right on Oakland St, then turn left onto a path. Follow the path over several dips, then turn right onto the Sudbury Aqueduct.
6. Turn right onto Brookside Ave.
7. Turn left onto Oakland St and ascend to Centennial Park.
8. Turn left into the park and descend to the parking area.
9. Complete the first half of the numbered loop, then follow the edge of a field uphill. At the corner of the field, enter the woods and follow the path uphill.
10. The path emerges from the woods at the top of another field. Descend through the field to the pond.
11. Double back to the road and run downhill to the start.

Notes: This run's Barbizonian views and reflective pools are a sound prescription for the jaded jogger. For a longer run, the Sudbury Aqueduct can be explored in both directions. If you prefer the streets, Forest St and Abbott Rd set the standard for haute-suburban-canopy-covered bliss.

Facilities: Restrooms and water are available at Marathon Sports on Route 16 (255 Washington St).

Map IV: *The Southwestern Suburbs*

3.9 miles

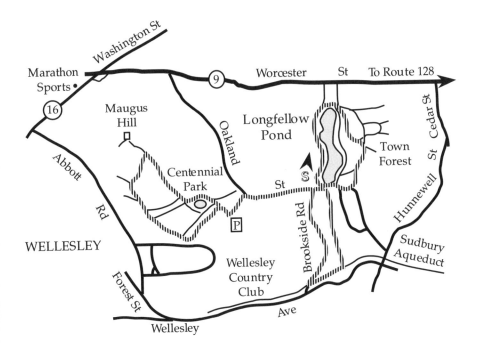

Hill Profile

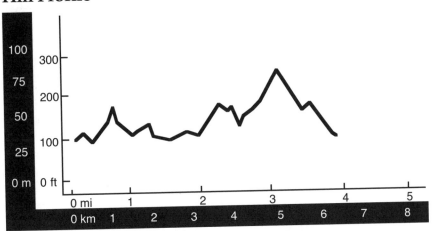

Lake Waban

Distances:	**Total Miles**	**8.1**
	North Loop	5.0
	South Loop	3.0

Surfaces: Paved pathway, sidewalk, and side of road.

Directions:
1. Start at Wellesley College.
2. Run east on Central St.
3. Turn right onto Grove St.
4. Turn right onto Charles River St.
5. Turn right onto Winding River Rd.
6. Continue on Winding River which becomes Livingston Rd.
7. Turn left onto Dover Rd.
8. Turn left onto Washington St.
9. Turn right onto Pond Rd.
10. Turn right onto Central St and return to the start.

Notes: Those who enjoy saving the best for last may agree that this loop is best run clockwise. Pond Rd has both the best scenery and steepest climbs. Of course, the rolling course makes plenty of demands before the difficult finish, so avoid burning up all your matches near the start. Lake Waban's dirt trails and Wellesley College's paved pathways are an attractive alternative to the sidewalks of Central and Washington Streets. Another popular Wellesley run is the Futter Brook trail which parallels Washington Street, passes by Wellesley High, and terminates near Route 9.

Facilities: Although busy, Central and Washington Streets are the best bets for finding restrooms and water.

8.1 miles

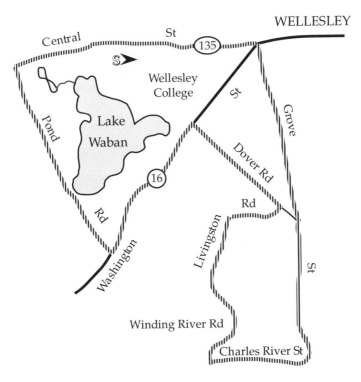

Hill Profile

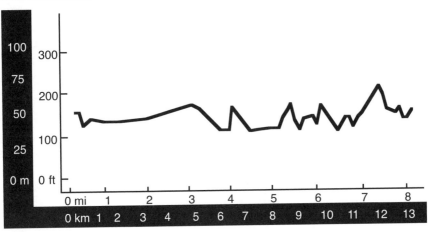

Elm Bank Reservation

Distances:	**Total Miles**	2.2

Surfaces: Trail and road.

Directions:
1. Elm Bank Reservation is located at 900 Washington St.
2. Cross bridge to Reservation.
3. Follow roads and trails around the park's perimeter.

Notes: The Charles River wraps around Elm Bank like a moat, and yet one hardly feels isolated among the Reservation's dedicated recreationalists: the soccer players, the dog-walkers, the canoers. Elm Bank is at once remote and accessible; hidden and popular; small and expandable. In fact, one or more laps at Elm Bank make an excellent warm up and cool down should you choose to combine the Reservation with longer runs such as Lake Waban [p. 106], Natick [p. 110], or Dover-Sherborn [p. 112].

Facilities: Reservation Headquarters' facilities, while historically available, were not open at the time of publication. A gas station is located roughly opposite the Reservation entrance on Washington St.

Map IV: The Southwestern Suburbs

2.2 miles

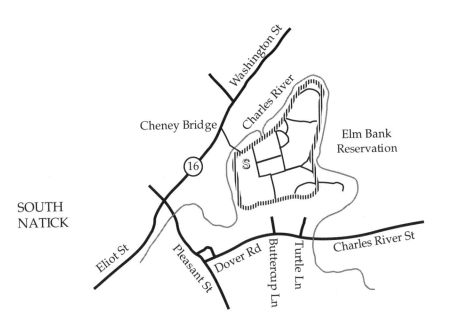

WELLESLEY

Washington St

Charles River

Cheney Bridge

Elm Bank
Reservation

16

S

SOUTH
NATICK

Eliot St

Pleasant St

Dover Rd

Buttercup Ln

Turtle Ln

Charles River St

DOVER

Natick

Distances:	**Total Miles**	**9.5**
	Union St Loop	7.3

Surfaces: Sidewalk and side of road.

Directions:
1. Start at the intersection of East Central and Union St.
2. Run south on Union St.
3. Turn right onto Woodland St.
4. Turn right onto Cottage St.
5. Turn left onto Farewell St.
6. Turn left onto Rockland St.
7. Turn left onto Everett St.
8. Merge left onto Eliot St (Route 16).
9. Turn left onto Pond St.
10. Turn right onto Central St.
11. Turn left (under overpass) onto Bacon St.
12. Turn left onto Marion St and descend hill to start.

Notes: How to Make a Hill Sandwich:

1. Marinate a flat slice of Route 16 in Charles River water, then steep in the quaintness of South Natick's Eliot Historic District.
2. Place the slice between the rolling hills of Woodland St and the bulkie-roll contours of Pond St.
3. Top it all off, of course, with Bacon St.
4. Slice it up according to your appetite using the Cottage and Union St shortcuts.

Facilities: Restrooms and water are available in businesses or public buildings (i.e. library, fire house) in South Natick.

Map IV: The Southwestern Suburbs

9.5 miles

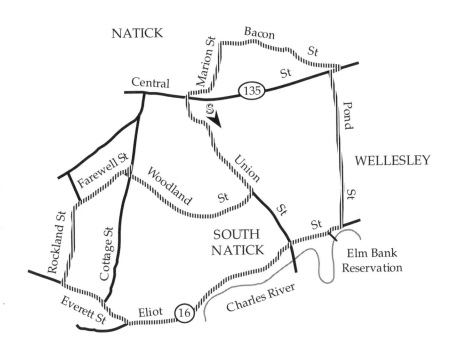

Hill Profile

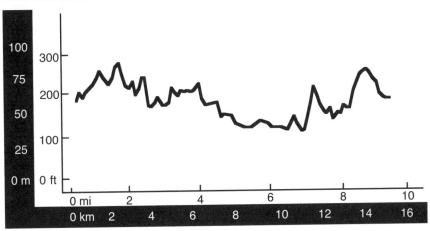

Dover-Sherborn

Distances:	**Total Miles**	**12.9**

Surfaces: Road and sidewalk. Trail optional.

Directions:
1. Start at intersection of Route 16 and Pleasant St.
2. Turn left onto Charles River St.
3. Turn right onto Centre St.
4. Turn right onto Springdale Ave.
5. Turn left onto Farm St.
6. Turn right onto Bridge St.
7. Turn left onto Forest St.
8. Turn right (hairpin) onto Lake St.
9. Turn right onto Farm Rd.
10. Turn left onto South St.
11. Turn right onto Route 16 and return to the start.

Notes: Beware of traffic on Farm St, for drivers--like runners--may find it difficult to suppress their enthusiasm for a fast romp over a winding country road. Two pleasant side excursions are available to a pair of well-trained legs. The first, Elm Bank Reservation [p. 108], lies north of Charles River St. The second, Sherborn Town Forest and Rocky Narrows Reservation, is accessible from the small parking area on Forest St. A detailed trail map is posted at the trail head.

Facilities: Restrooms and water are available on Lake St at the edge of Farm Pond, in businesses on Route 16, and at the South Natick Library near the start.

Map IV: The Southwestern Suburbs

12.9 miles

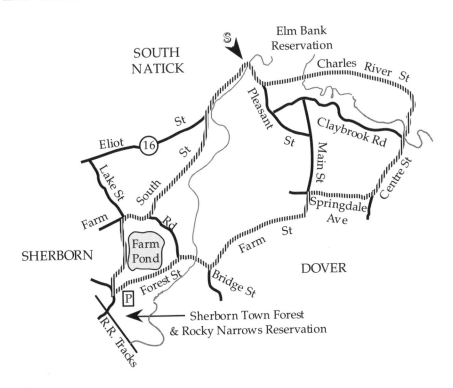

Hill Profile

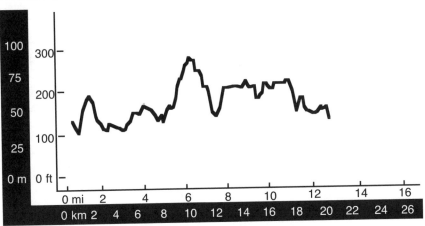

Ridge Hill

| Distances: | **Total Miles** | **2.6** |
| | To Needham Town Forest [p. 116] | 1.4 |

Surfaces: Trail.

Directions:
1. Ridge Hill Reservation is located off of Charles River St in the western corner of Needham.
2. Start at the Fit Trail near the parking area.
3. Follow the Fit Trail, and turn right onto Esker Trail.
4. Turn right onto Moonbeam Trail. [Note: the trail head, marked by two blue disks, appears after fitness stop #20].
5. Turn left back onto Esker. When the trail dips down, look right for the steps that descend the embankment to Swamp Trail. Turn right onto Swamp Trail.
6. After crossing a bridge, turn right onto Chestnut Trail.
7. Bear right onto North Trail and continue over the hill, past the turn-off for Drumlin Trail to the perimeter.
8. Follow the perimeter trail up the hill and continue down the opposite side. As you approach Charles River St, the path ducks left into the woods and returns to the start.

Notes: This run strings together much of Ridge Hill's natural diversity, but the freelance wanderer is sure to expose the author's glaring oversights. For example, by meandering along the Charles River Trail, one discovers Baker Brook. For a 7.4 mile run, combine this route with the Needham Town Forest run.

Facilities: Water is available next to the open field, and restrooms are adjacent to the picnic area.

2.6 miles

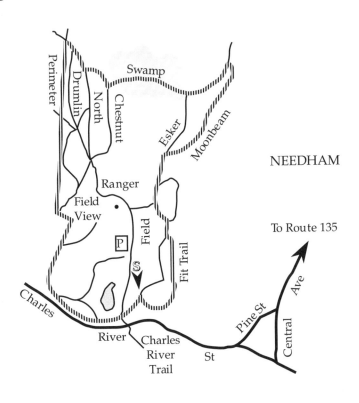

Hill Profile

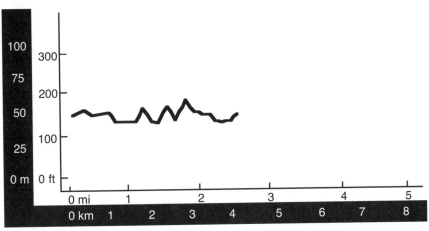

Needham Town Forest

| Distances: | **Total Miles** | 2.0 |
| | To Ridge Hill [p. 114] | 1.4 |

Surfaces: Trail and side of road.

Directions: 1. Start at parking area off Central Ave.
2. Run out of the back of the lot onto the central trail.
3. Bear right, left, and then right to reach the exit at Gatewood Dr.
4. Turn right on Gatewood Dr, and continue over the hill.
5. At White Pine Rd, turn left and return to the trails.
6. Follow trail back northward to close the loop.
7. Retrace the path to start.

Notes: The Town Forest is not pristine, but it has survived encroaching houses, a neighboring dump and heavy recreation. Here and there, one sees evidence of its toughness: dirt packed as hard as a turtle shell, bare-knuckled boulders poking through a tattered brown cape, and trails branching off a central spine like frayed nerves. Impulsive explorers should follow their hearts, but please tread lightly on the footpaths. The forest may put up a durable and resilient front, but its plants and critters can be extremely sensitive.

Facilities: The Town Forest has neither restrooms nor water fountains. However, the Ridge Hill run is less than a mile-and-a-half away.

Map IV: The Southwestern Suburbs

2.0 miles

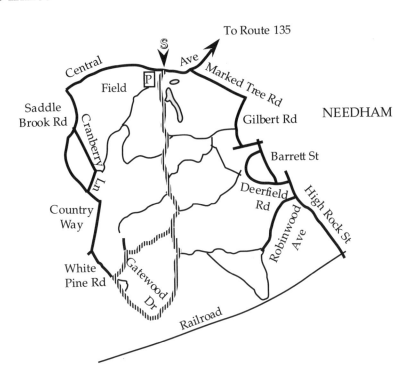

Hill Profile

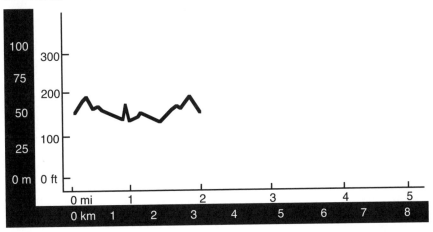

117

Boston Marathon®

Distances:	**Total Miles**	**26.2**

Surfaces: Sidewalk and side of road.

Directions: 1. Start at Hopkinton Common on Route 135 near Town Hall. (The start line is painted on the road).
2. Follow Route 135 east through Ashland, Framingham, Natick and into Wellesley.
3. Shortly after passing the halfway point near Wellesley Square, merge left onto Route 16 (Washington St).
4. Continue on Rte 16 through Wellesley; pass over Rte 128.
5. Turn right onto Route 30 (Commonwealth Ave).
6. Continue over Heartbreak Hill.
7. At the eastern end of the Reservoir, merge right onto Chestnut Hill Ave.
8. Turn left onto Beacon St. Continue past Coolidge Corner, Kenmore Square and Massachusetts Ave.
9. Turn right onto Hereford St.
10. Turn left onto Boylston St and continue to the finish at the Boston Public Library.

Notes: Yes, this can be a training run, but athletes who meet the time qualification standards for their age groups should enter to run the Marathon. The point-to-point course is more pleasant on Patriot's Day, when the streets close to traffic and supportive strangers hand out fuel and and drink. Without the race-day amenities, downtown Natick isn't nearly as cheerful, but some things never change: the finish is still sixteen miles away.

Facilities: Restrooms and water are available at Marathon Sports (near the 15 mile mark on Washington St). Gas stations and businesses also line the route.

Map IV: The Southwestern Suburbs

26.2 miles

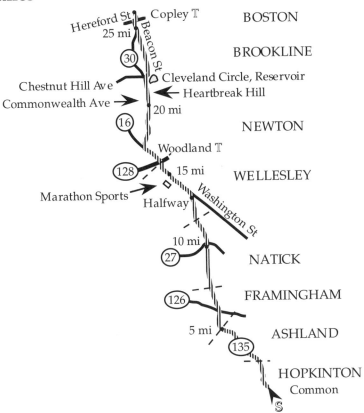

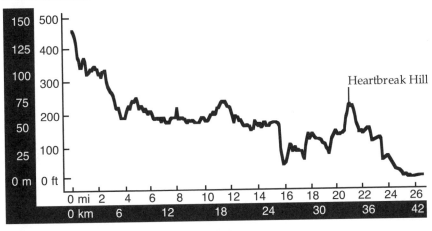

Hill Profile

I. Tracks

Access: the Inside Track

High school tracks are usually open to all-comers, and prohibitions on outsiders are rarely enforced. By contrast, most University tracks are formally limited to students, faculty, and alumni. Informally, visitors are usually tolerated so long as the school teams are not practicing. (Note that the most important rules are informal. For example, slower runners are usually expected to yield the inner lanes to faster runners). Runners may also gain track access through local running clubs or paid memberships. Because the indoor tracks are more closely guarded, indoor runners who are not associated with a school will probably have to buy a membership, join a club, or befriend a student.

The Closer the Better?

Although local high school tracks are usually the most convenient sites for speed works, many runners are willing to travel to club workouts. The competition and camaraderie of a club setting guard against staleness and boost performances. Convenience is good, but it's not always worth running on cinders or asphalt. You wouldn't be the first runner to wake up at six and bike across town in search of a soft artificial surface.

Outdoor:

Harvard, Soldiers Field
Access: limited; no visitors during team practice hours (3-6 P.M.).
Distance: 400m.
Surface: artificial all-weather, moderately hard, Dalton.
Track office: 617-495-2218

MIT
Access: limited; no visitors during team practice hours (5-7 P.M.).
The MIT-only policy is not currently enforced, but rates for membership are typically $40 per season.
Distance: 400 m.
Surface: artificial all-weather, firm, CA products.
Track office: 617-253-4918

Indoor:

Harvard, Soldiers Field
Gordon Indoor Track and Tennis
Access: limited.
Distance: 220 yd.
Information: 617-495-4205

Reggie Lewis Track Center
1350 Tremont St.
Access: 3 month membership for $55; one year membership for $200.
Distance: 220 yd.
Information: 617-541-3535

II. Seasonal Notes

Signs of Spring

Grass reappears between patches of snow, and the trails bog up like clam chowder. The sun may be pale, but if the *New England Runner* calendar is out, prime road-racing season can't be far off. Then, the March miracle unfolds as, one-by-one, the bubblers gurgle to life. Runners also surge back, sometimes risking injury to compensate for winter hibernations. In April, the Boston Marathon spills out of Hopkinton. The orb radiates back north, and runners peel off layers of laminated micro fibers.

Escape From Heat Island

Avoid water-loving cotton which tends to cling and chafe, but be a water-loving person and hydrate. Always run with water. Hydrate again. Consider a change of venue for very humid conditions. Early morning trail runs shade against the ultraviolet bake. Shoreline runs are invariably cooler than inland climes. Remember that Boston's heat-island effect and urban air quality can intensify any preexisting lethargy factor.

Fall Foliage

New England hits full stride: cross-country invades Franklin Park; distance runners flock to regional marathons. Trail runners enjoy every soft mushy stride amidst the foliage of Concord and Lincoln. Savor the perfect conditions while they last, and avoid over-dressing as the leaves begin to drop. Abandoning a warm bed for foul weather requires a leap of faith. Runners who trust that their bodies will generate thirty-or-so degrees of heat over the first few miles will avoid overheating. As of November, runners should prepare for the bone-chilling moment when they arrive a water fountain, turn the handle, and receive . . . not a drop.

Shorts Days, Long Season

While some runners escape to treadmills and indoor tracks, others look forward to winter running, snow-shoeing or nordic skiing. Snow itself is not the enemy; packed snow, while tough on calf muscles, is a decent running surface. Driving sleet and ice pose the biggest threats to warmth and stability. Anyone who hopes to "run through" should invest in technical clothing, reflective materials and a shoe with a grippy outsole. In the coldest weather, all skin surfaces--including extremities--should be covered. Some park areas, such as Fresh Pond, are well plowed. Moderately traveled roads often combine the benefits of decent surface quality (i.e. plowed, sanded or salted) with low-volume traffic.

III. Running Clubs

Eastern Massachusetts is home to a variety of running groups with memberships that mirror the diversity of the larger running community. Club runners range from the Olympic qualifier to the adventurer who risks the social mayhem of the Hash House Harrier runs. Club activity centers around mid-week track workouts and weekend long runs. Newcomers may join these sessions to decide which combination of coaching, competition and camaraderie best meets their needs.

Club and web address (http://)	Contact	Phone
Back Bay Road Runners	Don Allison	617-893-8383
Boston Athletic Association	Ed Sheehan	617-236-1652
www.baa.org or www.bostonmarathon.org		
Boston Hash House Harriers*	Hotline	617-499-4835
world.std.com/~twm3/bh3_home.html		
Boston Running Club	Rich Schilder	617-964-7802
www.brc.org		
Cambridge Running Club	Al Nagel	617-259-0148
www.tiac.net/users/b30845		
Cambridge Sports Union	Hotline	617-354-2786
world.std.com/~jwaldron/csu.htm		
Greater Boston Track Club	Tom Derderian	617-499-4844
www.research.digital.com/CRL/personal/tuttle/gbtc/home.html		
Greater Framingham Track Club	Thomas Abbott	508-651-3322
Greater Lowell Road Runners	Hotline	508-937-5221
www.coolrunning.com/club/glrr.htm		
Irish American Track Club (Medford)	Wesley Foote	617-396-5487
Liberty Athletic Club	Kathy Nary	508-463-0597
A competitive, all-women's running club.		
L-Street Running Club (S. Boston)	John McDermott	617-331-1761
Lynn Athletic Club	Bob Levine	617-598-0395
Merrimack Valley Striders (Andover)	Hotline	508-687-8887
www1.usa1.com/~dsmith		
North Medford Club	Ken Robichaud	508-345-6042
North Shore Striders (Marblehead)	Gary Freedman	617-631-5442
Parkway Running Club (W. Roxbury)	Jon Connor	617-469-3448
www.research.digital.com/CRL/personal/tuttle/gbtc/westroxbury.html		
Somerville Road Runners	Robert Coburn	617-391-1237
web.mit.edu/rcharbon/Public/www/srr.html		
South Shore YMCA (Quincy)	Gayle Laing	617-479-8500
Tri-Valley Frontrunners (Milford)	Frank Nealon	508-376-8660
Whirlaway Racing Team (Methuen)	David Kazanjian	508-688-8356
Winner's Circle Running Club (Salisbury)	Mike McCormick	508-462-0117

* "The drinking club with the running problem."

IV. Resources

Running Specialty Stores

◇ Bill Rodgers Running Center
Faneuil Hall Market Place
353-T North Market Place; Boston, MA 02109; 617-723-5612
◇ Marathon Sports
1654 Mass Ave.; Cambridge, MA 02138; 617-354-4161
255 Washington St.; Wellesley Hills, MA 02181; 617-237-0771
◇ Runner's Edge (www.runedge.com)
401 Main St; Melrose, MA 02176; 617-662-0091
◇ The Front Runner
1072 Main St (Route 109); Millis, MA 02054; 508-376-8660

USA Track and Field-New England

2001 Beacon St, Suite 207
mailing address: PO Box 1905; Brookline, MA 02146; 617-566-7600

Internet Resources

The Internet is an explosive source of information and commerce. It is also a dynamic medium that links runners to one another for advice, debate, discussion and support. Explore running links using the following addresses as points of departure.

Regional Web Sites and Addresses (http://)

MDC Reservations	www.magnet.state.ma.us/mdc/reserv.htm
Mass. Forests and Parks	www.magnet.state.ma.us/dem/toc.htm
Globe Corner Bookstores	www.gcb.com/catalog/ or 1-800-358-6013
Coolrunning	www.coolrunning.com
New England Runner	www.runningnetwork.com/nerunner
Hockomock Swamp Rat	www.channel1.com/users/mcwall/

Other Internet Resources

Dead Runner's Society	storm.cadcam.iupui.edu/drs/drs.html
Running Network	www.runningnetwork.com
Endurance Training Journal	s2.com/etj/
Runner's World	www.runnersworld.com/
Runners Web	www.sirius.on.ca/running.html
The Running Page	sunsite.unc.edu/drears/running/running.html
Running on the Web	sorrel.humboldt.edu/~rrw1/runweb.html
Yahoo running directory	www.yahoo.com/recreation/sports/running
Usenet Newsgroup (news:)	rec.running

Afterword

I wrote this book out of a desire to share my experiences on local roads and trails. I wanted to put together the most comprehensive guide available on the subject. However, given the vast number of running adventures available in the Boston area, this book exposes no more than the tip of the iceberg. Having limited the scope of this edition to fifty runs, I faced many tough decisions about which routes to include.

Omissions were made based on considerations of traffic, accessibility, usefulness, geographical distribution, and other factors. For example, I did not include several shoreline destinations such as Swampscott, Revere, and Hull, assuming that most runners would anticipate the scenic vistas, salty breezes, and generally flat topography. Other economies were more arbitrary. A few exceptional runs fell victim to limited space. A partial list might include Horn Pond (Woburn), Truman Hwy and Brush Hill Road (Hyde Park, Milton), Noanet Woodlands (Dover), Great Brook Farm State Park (Carlisle), Futter Brook Trail (Wellesley), Needham Reservoir, VFW Parkway and Stony Brook Reservation (West Roxbury), and many others.

I'd be delighted to hear your ideas for subsequent editions. Tell me which information was particularly useful, or offer your suggestions for improvement. Where road and trail conditions have changed, please send me your clarifications or corrections. Please do not hesitate to propose either an embellishment to an existing run or the inclusion of your own favorite routes. Thanks!

Address all correspondence to:

Editor, *Running In and Around Boston*
Ouizel Books
P.O. Box 2007
Osterville, MA 02655

To request more information or to place an order, write to Ouizel Books, or
CALL TOLL-FREE: 1-888-WILD-RUN
Discounts are available for bulk sales.